EDUCATION IS FREEDOM

The Future Is in Your Hands

JAMES W. KEYES

SAVIO REPUBLIC

CW01645701

A SAVIO REPUBLIC BOOK
An Imprint of Post Hill Press
ISBN: 979-8-88845-747-4
ISBN (eBook): 978-1-63758-801-7

Education Is Freedom:
The Future Is in Your Hands
© 2024 by James W. Keyes
All Rights Reserved

Cover Design by Jim Villaflores

All Scripture quotations, unless otherwise indicated, are taken from the Holy Bible, New International Version®, NIV®. Copyright ©1973, 1978, 1984, 2011 by Biblica, Inc.™ Used by permission of Zondervan. All rights reserved worldwide. www.zondervan.com The "NIV" and "New International Version" are trademarks registered in the United States Patent and Trademark Office by Biblica, Inc.™

Scripture taken from the New King James Version®. Copyright © 1982 by Thomas Nelson. Used by permission. All rights reserved.

No part of this book may be reproduced, stored in a retrieval system, or transmitted by any means without the written permission of the author and publisher.

SAVIO REPUBLIC

posthillpress.com
New York • Nashville
Published in the United States of America

1 2 3 4 5 6 7 8 9 10

To my father, who taught me to fish.

Mankind must *Live to Learn...*

Before we will *Learn to Live*

TABLE OF CONTENTS

Foreword by Stedman Graham 9
Introduction - A Handbook for Humanity 13

SECTION I
LIVING TO LEARN

Chapter 1 - Education IS Freedom: Finding the Spark 21
Chapter 2 - The State of Education: Making the System Work for YOU 36
Chapter 3 - Living the Dream: Unlocking Your Future 57
Chapter 4 - Nothing to Fear: Light the Darkness with Knowledge 69

SECTION II
WHAT TO LEARN

Chapter 5 - Change: Change Equals Opportunity 87
Chapter 6 - Confidence: Know You Can 99
Chapter 7 - Clarity: Keep it Simple…Smart! 117

SECTION III
HOW TO LEARN

Chapter 8 - Critical Thinking: Understanding Your "Why" 133
Chapter 9 - Curiosity: Jet Fuel for Learning 145
Chapter 10 - Creativity: Intelligence at Play 157

SECTION IV

WHY WE LEARN

Chapter 11 - Collaboration: Bigger than Thyself 175

Chapter 12 - Cultural Literacy: Weaving Your Quilt of Diversity 191

Chapter 13 - Character: You Are What You Believe 205

SECTION V

LEARNING TO LIVE

Chapter 14 - Technology: The Great Enabler 225

Chapter 15 - Lifelong Learning: Becoming a Renaissance Person 239

Chapter 16 - Wisdom: The Rx for Humanity 253

Acknowledgments 267

About the Author 269

FOREWORD

By Stedman Graham
Bestselling Author, Businessman, and Speaker

Sitting at a dinner, over twenty years ago, I found that the gentleman seated next to me shared a common interest in education. The words he shared with me during that dinner caught my attention. He boldly proclaimed: "*Education is Freedom*!" Here was this CEO, the leader of one of the world's most recognizable brands, 7-Eleven, acknowledging the power of education to change the world. That day, Jim Keyes and I became fast friends. We shared a love for education and a belief that everyone, armed with a good education, can accomplish anything in this wonderful world in which we live.

I later discovered that Jim and I share many other interests including the great game of golf. On the course, I found that despite his kindness and benevolence, he was one competitive guy. He is indeed a fierce but fun competitor. Of the many talents he has, there is one that has always stood out—his determination to make things happen. Looking back at his career, he is clearly a man that rose to face a tremendous challenge. Dedicated to his purpose and cause, Jim would always follow through and deliver on the goals that he set. This book is no different. Writing a book is not easy. In fact, it is probably one of the most difficult challenges a person can take on. I applaud him for seeing this process through and bringing this important message to the world. With this book, he is now able to share his remarkable insight into the power of education.

But that is just one medium to share his love of education with the world. Jim is also the founder of the Education is Freedom Foundation. I had the privilege of serving for many years as a founding member on the organization's board of directors and continue to be proud of the work they have done. The foundation has changed hundreds of thousands of lives by helping young people understand the value of education and believe in their own ability to navigate an educational journey. For many years, I encouraged Jim to expand the reach of this important initiative. That is the foundation on which Jim built *Education Is Freedom*.

Jim continues to support many other organizations that focus on helping people succeed. He is an amazing presenter and speaker, and now, through this book, he can share his personal and professional message with a much wider, even worldwide, audience. I am confident you will enjoy it and learn a great deal from Jim's humble upbringing and remarkable professional and personal accolades.

Jim is, and always has been, committed to the belief that every person—especially in America—deserves an education. Armed with that education, anything is possible. That message is more important now than at any other time in our history. We have experienced the Industrial Age and the Machine Age. Now, we are in the Information Age. Today, we have so much access to this information. There has never been a better time for advancement. When we learn how to take such content and apply it to our talents, skills, and abilities—the things that make us who we are—we can achieve amazing results.

Living in America offers us so many opportunities and resources. But we lessen those possibilities without a solid education. When I was younger, I wish I would have understood the value and importance of education. I wish I recognized how it could change your life. Luckily, it is never too late. I realize that today and find myself trying to make up for lost time. If we could share this understanding with every young person across the globe, then we can rescue them from their own self-doubt. We can empower them with a belief in the power of learning to overcome obstacles and unlock opportunity. What if we could share this message with the world. When we help even one child, we help the entire community. Well now we can help all of humanity, by spreading the word about *Education Is Freedom*!

We can all be reminded of the power of learning to transform lives…even our own.

This is why I am very excited about Jim's work and commitment to empowering people to recognize that *education* really is *freedom*. It is an honor and a pleasure to be part of this movement.

INTRODUCTION

A HANDBOOK FOR HUMANITY

Whatever the circumstances of your birth, none of us are born free. Freedom is something we learn. As a child, we could not survive alone in the jungle or on the streets. We need to learn to have the necessities of survival. That reality doesn't change as we age. We must *learn* to be free. This doesn't mean simply learning the basics. Yes, we all must learn to read, write, and do basic arithmetic. But learning doesn't stop there. True freedom requires that we continue to learn and grow our knowledge. As we will find, knowledge alone isn't enough. We must also develop wisdom for our personal growth and for the future of mankind. The more we learn, as individuals and as one people living together on this planet earth, the more freedom we can enjoy.

But what is freedom? Today, the word *freedom* is front and center in the headlines. To some it means freedom of speech or freedom of religion. To others it might mean freedom from discrimination. To the avid outdoorsman, it might be the freedom to bear arms. To others it might be freedom to marry the person of one's choice. When difficult choices must be made, our individual pursuit of freedom may at times conflict with the freedoms of others. In the extreme, one person's definition of freedom may be seen as another person's fascism and maybe yet another person's communism. For true freedom to exist in any form, within any society, there is one common denominator. Individuals must be able to make informed choices and informed decisions. Therefore *knowledge* is a prerequisite for freedom to exist. Beyond simple knowledge, our *wisdom* is essential for freedom to thrive. This, of course, is *why* education is freedom!

The pages ahead will trace the pathway for education to develop our individual and collective *wisdom*. Along the way, we will address the *what, how,* and *why* of learning. You may already know much of what you might discover in these pages, but it is intended to serve as a reminder or an awakening of the critical success factors that help us learn. The objective is, very simply, to inspire us all to learn and to keep learning because *wisdom* (a higher degree of knowledge) is the lifeblood of a civil society and the oxygen that fuels our personal enlightenment.

To my young readers: the future is yours. I encourage you to fuel your dreams with learning. There is much debate in recent years about the importance of college or advanced education. Don't be fooled. The more you learn, the more you can do. Whether a trade that requires vocational training or a professional career that requires a graduate degree, continued learning is essential to be the best at what you do. The more you learn, the more freedom you will enjoy to pursue your dreams.

To those in the first third of life's journey: it is never too late to embrace change. Learning allows you to change your trajectory to achieve your dreams. If you're trapped in a job that doesn't fulfill you or if you're ready to pursue an additional degree, the more you are able to learn the more opportunity you will enjoy. This book will impart the confidence you need to embrace change and course correct. Know that it is never, ever too late!

For those in the second two thirds of their lives: let this work be a reminder that it is never too late to learn. Whether a new hobby, a new language, or a new career later in life, the more we learn, the more we can live. The more we as individuals can reignite our fundamental learning skills, the more we will collectively contribute to society. The future of freedom depends on it.

From the first moments of putting pen on paper, I hoped to make this book an extension of my dream in building the Education is Freedom Foundation. That dream is a lifelong mission to help each of us recognize our full potential by taking advantage of the power of education to improve our lives and the lives of those around us. My mission is to inspire readers to believe in themselves and address the *what, how, and why* of education.

In the pages to follow, you'll find personal anecdotes from my own journey, and the experiences of friends and those throughout history who have successfully used education to change their own life and to enrich the lives of others. It is not a memoir, but instead intended to provide examples from my life journey to show what is possible even with seemingly impossible odds. It is intended to inspire others to accomplish the impossible and to use education as their path to freedom.

My dream is to enable more people to use education as their path to success. If you agree with this goal, then I hope you'll see *Education Is Freedom* as a book to be given to anyone who wishes to succeed in their learning journey. While the goal is that *Education Is Freedom* becomes a beacon of hope for students to believe in themselves and their ability to fulfill their full destiny through education, the dream doesn't stop there. There is a broader audience that I hope this book will inspire.

The broader audience is all of us, society at large. As a people, we owe the general advancement of the human condition today to the growth of knowledge over the centuries. Most of the issues that we grapple with today from crime to personal safety; from hunger to malnutrition; from terrorism to war are all problems that can be improved if not eradicated through the power of knowledge. The future of humanity will hinge on our continued growth of individual and collective knowledge. With this objective, *Education Is Freedom* is a timely handbook for humanity.

Our founding fathers understood that *only* an educated populace could make the American experiment in self-government succeed. Thomas Jefferson believed that the very cornerstone of our democracy would rest on the foundation of an educated electorate. "If a nation expects to be ignorant and free, in a state of civilization," he said, "it expects what never was and never will be." Throughout history, the two-party system in our democracy has maintained a healthy debate over two sides of virtually every issue. Today, that debate has often become less than healthy, degenerating into polarized positions with an absence of civil discourse. The importance of embracing what I call the "C-Suite of Learning: *change, confidence, clarity, critical thinking, curiosity, creativity, collaboration, cultural literacy, and character*," are all essential to enhance our democratic process.

One thing both parties have in common is a fundamental belief in the importance of education to the preservation of freedom. Ronald Reagan once said, "If America is to offer greater economic opportunity to her citizens, if she's to defend our freedom, democracy, and keep the peace, then our children will need wisdom, courage, and strength—virtues beyond their reach without education." John F. Kennedy, who inspired the country to put a man on the moon, said that "our progress as a nation can be no swifter than our progress in education. The human mind is our fundamental resource."

President Kennedy's speech held a bold challenge in September 1962 at Rice University in Houston: "We choose to go to the moon in this decade and do the other things, not because they are easy, but because they are hard." Seven years later, while at a Boy Scout Camp called Treasure Valley, I watched Buzz Aldrin and Neil Armstrong become the first men to walk on the moon.

Few of us have been blessed with the ability to call an Apollo astronaut, "my friend Buzz." I have had that blessing. Little did I know that many years later I would be on stage with Buzz, being inducted into the Horatio Alger Association of Distinguished Americans. Since meeting Buzz, I've enjoyed the incredible privilege of flying with him and other Apollo astronauts like Walt Cunningham of Apollo 7, Al Worden of Apollo 15, and Charlie Duke of Apollo 16 as copilots in the cockpit of an aircraft with the time to discuss life and its many challenges. There is one common denominator amongst these great American heroes—they have seen the Earth from a different vantage point. Looking back on the Earth from space, they saw the most beautiful planet imaginable. They didn't see borders, the Vietnam War in progress, the demonstrations back home, the racism tearing people apart, or the poverty gripping entire nations. Not in the least.

Rather, the beautiful planet they saw before them was home. They saw fellow earthlings...not races, not ideologies, not religions, and not gender. They saw fellow inhabitants of this beautiful planet Earth, one planet, under God, indivisible. They saw that knowledge made it possible for mankind to travel beyond the gravitational pull of Earth, and that education made it possible for them as individuals to have the privilege of making that journey. A common denominator among all who have seen this planet from space is that we are all in this together, as one people, and our individual and collective education will continue to make this world a better place.

In the future, perhaps we will all one day enjoy this "world view," but meanwhile we should all recognize the power of education to bring us together as one people. Every future astronaut who walks across the campus of the Air Force Academy will see a statue with a plaque that reads: "Man's flight through life is sustained by the power of his knowledge." May the following pages provide tailwinds and some additional lift for your flight through life.

MAN'S FLIGHT
THROUGH LIFE IS
SUSTAINED BY THE
POWER OF HIS
KNOWLEDGE.

SECTION I
LIVING TO LEARN

As infants, we first learned to crawl and then to walk. Through knowledge, humans learned to drive and even to fly. Yet, we only learn to soar through wisdom. Learning powers our journey through life, but the wisdom from that learning allows us to soar as free as an eagle above the rest. We can choose to live a simple life, learning only what we need to survive. Or, we can pursue a path of lifelong learning and enjoy all that this wonderful life has to offer. The choice is yours.

In your flight through life, education is the wind beneath your wings. Each of us is blessed with a beautiful mind that can elevate us beyond our imagination. From the first hours of consciousness, our mind begins the slow process of learning and developing the programming that guides our dreams, our abilities, our experiences, and ultimately our destiny. Learning then becomes a lifelong endeavor. But it is one that comes with a choice—to be passive observers and allow this programming to be influenced by what we see and hear alone or to be active programmers that seek knowledge to help us grow.

Our environment and upbringing may influence this choice. Our socioeconomic reality, family circumstances, or any number of factors can impact our potential, but rarely defines it. The obstacles are many and the excuses are easy. To some, it may seem impossible because there is always someone or something in the way, seemingly trying to hold us down or take away what we have. No one can take away what you learn, what you know, and what you understand. It is, in many respects, the only true wealth that we have while on this earth. We can then turn this true wealth of knowledge into material benefits and enjoy a life of luxury, or we can use it to enrich the lives of others. The choice is yours, but the simple truth is that education will provide more options and more choices.

If you *live to learn*...then you will be on your way toward *learning to live.*

CHAPTER 1

EDUCATION IS FREEDOM: FINDING THE SPARK

"Education is the key to unlock the golden door of freedom."

George Washington Carver

Lifelong learning is a journey. It begins with curiosity, so join me by putting your curiosity into high gear. Let's take a few steps together. During this one small segment of your lifelong journey, we will explore many tales of adventure, opportunity, and, most importantly, freedom. This freedom isn't exclusive to one person, one sex, one race, or even one country. It is a story of freedom and opportunity that we can share and replicate. It can be *your* story. It can be *our* story.

Let's begin with an example: the story of a young child whose experience many millions of children across the globe have endured. Growing up without running water with a wood-burning stove and little to eat, the child could be in the streets of Brazil, the outback of Australia, or the wilds of Africa. Instead, this little boy grew up in a small town in central Massachusetts in a family with too little money and too many children to feed. The child's father and grandfather built the family's simple frame house on a humble plot of land. They didn't get around to installing plumbing or central heat but hoped to afford it one day. The challenges of that life were too much for the young boy's mother, who left for another man and the "luxury" of a mobile home. The little boy struggled to understand his mother's unhappiness. The place wasn't fancy, but it was home.

There were no expectations of the child beyond staying out of trouble or one day securing a job at the local factory. His brothers, sisters, aunts, uncles, and pretty much everyone in this small mill town had followed a similar career trajectory. Many of the boy's friends and family quit school, married early, and worked in the factory. His siblings all encouraged their younger brother to pursue a different path. His parents didn't know how or why, but they too agreed that education would change his life. It did. We all have a story, but this one was mine.

I was that little boy, and somehow managed to beat the odds. My father often said, "Get an education, son. It's the only thing they can't take away from you." I always wondered about this fatalistic advice but have heard many others echo it over the years. Why was my father so negative about those who would try to take something away? Why was he frustrated with his life? In my young eyes, he had it all—a home, a great kid to have as his sidekick, a car, a job in the local factory, and all the food and drink he needed. What more could one want?

True, we lacked running water in the house, but the pump outside delivered some of the coldest, freshest water I've ever tasted. True, we lacked a few creature comforts like central heat or air conditioning, but the wood-burning stove made it quite toasty during winter and the screens on our windows allowed for a nice breeze in the summer. What, I wondered, did my dad feel we were missing?

I remember asking him this once while fishing for lake trout at a local pond: "What more do you want, Dad? Is it money or things that we need to make us happy?"

He paused, surprised I had asked such a deep question. "No, son," he said. "It is freedom. I want the freedom to travel, the freedom to show you the world and to open your eyes to new opportunities and new adventures. The world is a glorious place, and I feel that we are trapped in part by my job and by the need to focus on necessities to live. I don't need money to be happy, but I do need freedom. I want that freedom for you, son. I wish I could show you the path, but I don't know how. All I know is that education seems to be the one common denominator that separates those who are free from those who are trapped in their own reality. Someone can take your money, your things, or your job, but they can't take away what you know. With that knowledge, you can replace anything lost, you can be free to explore the world, and you will be beholden to no one. It is freedom, son, that you should seek, and the absolute key to freedom is to learn as much as you can, every day of your life."

I didn't understand this advice, but I did take to heart the importance of education. Beyond the words of my father, I didn't have much else for inspiration. No one in my immediate family went on to college. Making it through high school, getting a job, and having a family became the typical path in our small factory town. Even among my extended family, only one uncle (my father's brother) had a college degree, and he went on to become a high school teacher in North Adams, Massachusetts.

I remembered trips to his North Adams home, a special treat during fall foliage season when the trees of the Berkshire Mountains would explode with color and the apples were crisp to the bite. His majestic home with running water and central heating featured an impressive library. As a child, the ability to afford a house with running water and the presence of books became my standard for "success." Many years later, I would be shocked to return to his modest frame home, having remembered it as a palatial estate. When I asked Uncle Leonard to see his "library," he had no idea what I meant. He took me to the small laundry room and pointed to a bookshelf above the washer/dryer. "This is the only place I've ever kept my books in this house," he told me.

That was the "library," a small shelf in the washroom, but through the eyes of a child this modest collection of books represented the key to knowledge and a ticket to success. It doesn't take much to inspire a child or to leave a lasting impression. In comparison to my dad, his brother enjoyed far more freedom. As a teacher, he took summers off and traveled the world. He wasn't trapped at a factory or forced to work at a machine for long hours every day. I wanted that kind of freedom. I didn't know the secret, or even the path, but I saw books as the portal. Through books I believed I could achieve freedom. I took seriously my father's admonition to learn, so I buried myself in books. They were my escape. They held the secrets of the universe and the key to independence. This was my spark!

This spark opened my eyes to the power of knowledge to change your quality of life. The real richness of life comes from experience not from money. I was fortunate to discover this at an early age. As a child, I didn't understand the difference between rich and poor. In my rural yard, filled with junk cars that my father would spend weekends tearing apart for scrap metal, my friends all found adventure. Together, we climbed on top of the cars and sat for hours inside, using our imaginations to create a fantasy environment, pretending to drive cross country together in one of those rusted-out vessels without an engine. My friends from the wealthy side of town had game rooms filled with the newest toys and technology, but their preference was to come to my place where they could run free. They had rules, they had constraints, and they had obligations to fulfill. I had poverty, but I didn't know it.

One Christmas, a well-dressed woman brought a basket of food to our house. I asked my grandmother why. She explained that the church was delivering food to the poor. I didn't understand. We weren't poor; we were rich. We had food, even if it was the blocks of government surplus cheddar cheese. We had water, even if it was from an outside well. We had freedom. I could *feel* the difference between our freedom and the constraints that others seemed to have. Of course, I didn't understand it nor could I explain it, but I knew there was a difference. I came to know at a very early age that freedom had little to do with money or things but instead had everything to do with life's experiences. I also learned that life's experiences come in all different shapes and sizes.

I knew things that these children, my peers in age but not experience, had been sheltered from. I knew about divorce. My parents separated when I was five. I knew about mortality. My father, who was my best friend and fishing buddy, passed away from cancer when I was twelve. I knew about dislocation. Walking home from my sixth-grade class, I found a sign that read "*condemned*" tacked on the door of our modest home, forcing me to live with my mother in her trailer home. I knew about abuse. Trying to find a better life for us, my mother moved us into a small home with her boyfriend. He was a master at physical and mental abuse. I knew about fear. While others dismissed my fear as irrational, I was honestly afraid he would try to kill me in my sleep. I knew about mental illness. After one of the nightly heated quarrels, I heard a car start in the basement garage of his home. Unsure of what was going on, I ran downstairs, only to discover him unconscious in his own car in a carbon monoxide–filled garage after he attempted to take his own life. I knew about survival. I knew that no one was going to take care of me if I didn't first take care of myself.

Despite those many challenges, I learned that adversity gave me strength. It made me tougher than my peers. When they fell off their bikes, they would run home crying. I had no one to run home to. Of course, I felt disadvantaged at times. I would sometimes ask, "Why me, Lord?" I would look around at many of my friends and wonder why they had such wonderful homes, clean clothes, and people to take care of them. But they were different. I found that many were soft. I didn't see the grit, the drive, and the determination. I saw fear, and I saw weakness. They were well cared for, but I was free. Was I free in a literal sense? Of course not; because of financial constraints, I had more limitations and restrictions than most of my peers. I knew that I wanted more for my own life and developed a thirst for knowledge. As I saw it, the more I knew, the more I *could* do. My father taught me to fish, literally. While other parents gave their child fish on a plate, my father taught me to catch them. And catch them I did. If I had a rod and a body of water, no one was going hungry on my watch.

It took many years to realize that adversity was an advantage. It gave me strength and a higher sense of awareness of the world around me. In many ways, it gave me freedom. My freedom came from within. I was free from the inside out. I was free in my mind, and that sense of freedom turned into a life of learning. That life of learning turned into a life of adventure and the foundation for this book.

Despite the hostile environment or constant challenges of a broken home, quickly I learned that success breeds success. As my grades improved due to my obsession with books, so did the encouragement. Teachers all provided strong support to promote my continued progress despite my tattered clothes and lack of personal hygiene. Without running water in the home, my first "bath" occurred at a relative's house at the age of ten. I wanted a better life for myself, so I invested even more deeply in my education.

I embraced learning. Taking on music, art, languages, and even athletics filled me with a love of adventure. Every new skill became a new love affair. A love of art gave me more to share with a new group of friends. A love of music led to jobs playing the organ at church services and weddings. A love of athletics taught me the importance of teamwork and kept me physically and mentally fit. Participation in the theater gave me a sense of confidence on stage that would become valuable for public speaking later. A love of life came from the study of humanities and a growing love for my fellow citizens of this Earth.

Any academic success I enjoyed did not materialize because of natural ability but because of my commitment to hard work. I may not have been smarter than anyone else in class, but I was determined to outwork them. This academic determination led to success throughout my educational journey, which included degrees from the College of the Holy Cross and the Columbia School of Business and a year abroad at the University of London. The combination of this academic journey and a commitment to hard work created career opportunities. In less than twenty years post-graduation, I had the privilege of leading two iconic brands. The first: as CEO of 7-Eleven, I oversaw a global public company and iconic brand with more than forty thousand stores. Then, I served as Chairman and CEO of Blockbuster. Education clearly fueled this odds-defying journey. Looking back, I realized that if I could do this, then anyone could. I've spent much of my life sharing the message that education combined with lifelong learning is the pathway to freedom. Despite obstacles, hurdles, and challenges, learning is at our fingertips and available to us all.

This awakening to the power of learning is certainly not new. Nelson Mandela called education "the most powerful weapon which you can use to change the world." His dear friend Oprah Winfrey has echoed these words, saying that education "is the key to unlocking the world, a passport to freedom." I had heard these words of wisdom, but they didn't sink in until a fateful encounter occurred one day on the Columbia University campus. I had been invited back to the business school to guest lecture for a course on leadership. Walking across campus in a suit and tie, briefcase in hand, a sense of pride and accomplishment welled up in me. Feeling a bit full of myself, I encountered a young man as he left the business school. The young African-American student, arms full of books, sported a T-shirt that stopped me in my tracks.

Three simple words blared from his shirt: "Education Is Freedom." The brilliance of these three words was life changing. I caught his attention, shook his hand, and introduced myself. I explained that his T-shirt had made an impression. I told him: "That's me! *I* am a product of education. Education *is* my freedom and has changed my life...so I'm grateful to you for proudly wearing that shirt and opening my eyes to this reality...that I am who I am, what I am, and where I am because of education, and I will be forever grateful for that awareness."

Encountering that young man changed my life. In that moment, a realization set in: my education wasn't over; it was just beginning. It dawned on me that I carried each lesson I had learned in a toolbox, and I could retrieve those lessons at will and place new lessons in the box. That chance encounter led me to become even more committed to lifelong learning and the opportunities that education can provide. I also became committed to sharing this awareness with others, to pay it forward by making everyone, young and old, understand that education is the path to individual freedom and, in a broader context, the freedom of all humankind. If I could do it, then clearly anyone could!

As simple as it may seem, if education is freedom, then freedom is powered by education. Since the beginning of time, both education and freedom began with the individual. Society (or humanity as I like to call it) is simply the cumulative reflection of the individuals within it. If we live in a society filled with uneducated individuals, then we cannot exist in a world of democratic self-determination and true freedom cannot exist. That then leads to three extremely important questions to address:

1. *Why must we learn?* Learning is life and growth. We must learn to collaborate to be productive members of society; to understand and appreciate cultural diversity; and to recognize that our character or identity is what we become to the world we face.

2. *How do we learn?* The basic formula for learning hasn't really changed since the beginning of time. As humans, our mind is capable of critical thinking. But that skill often goes unexercised. Driving critical thinking is our native

curiosity that makes us look around and wonder "why." Sprinkle in some creativity, and we are ready to have fun while learning.

3. *What must we learn?* Before beginning to learn, we must discard the obstacles of our own development. The ability to adapt to change, the confidence to do something about it, and the clarity to see through the darkness to the light and beyond are all things we must learn to do before we can begin our true learning journey.

Education has influenced each of our lives since birth. Whether it be in a traditional classroom setting or the kind of education you "experience"—street smarts, teamwork, relationships, and so much more—our individual and collective education is literally a cornerstone of society and crucial to our very existence.

Even though education is nearly everywhere we look, few speak of it in its most vital sense—as a path to freedom. That's right, education can set you free; free you of boundaries, of limiting beliefs, of poverty, of adversity, of poor influences, of scarcity of any kind. Education, in its many forms, is a life-changing and world-shaping solution that we often ignore because it is so obvious in all its elegant simplicity. Education *is* freedom!

If you love the idea of being free, it is vital that you understand what it means to be free. Freedom is often a misunderstood word, and to further complicate things, it has taken on a new meaning in recent times. We all know that freedom is, fundamentally, a "right or privilege." It is "the state or quality of being free" which means "exemption or liberation from the control of some other person or some arbitrary power." It means liberty. It means independence. It means the ability to control your destiny. This Collins Dictionary definition sounds quite simple on its face, but the concept of freedom is far more complex.

Freedom is an elusive dream *because* it eludes definition. It represents an internal conflict between free will and societal order. As such, the entire concept of freedom starts with an internal desire for free will and a willingness to do whatever it takes to balance that free will with whatever constraints the world around us may present. Free will begins with us, individually, in our thoughts and in our words. No one can give you freedom as it is something, like one's faith or inner peace, that must come from within. A prisoner in chains may have lost his physical liberty, but no one can control his mind, his dreams, and his free will to think and dream.

Since self-determination begins with "thyself," it should be logical that we must take responsibility for our own freedom. Because we are not alone in this world, our freedom also comes with a responsibility to others that we all must accept and exercise with the highest degree of accountability. No one will "make" us free or "set" us free. Freedom is a destiny that you choose and comes with a responsibility to yourself AND to others.

CREATING YOUR DESTINY: C-SUITE LEARNINGS

It took many years for my own road map to freedom to come into focus. Strangely enough, that awareness first occurred in the framework of a dream. Early in my career, I had one of those crazy early-morning dreams that make you want to leap out of bed and write down what you just experienced. In the dream, I was to receive a gift. It was the gift of life, of mindfulness, or as I like to say, the gift of freedom. To earn this gift I was asked to perform three different tasks. After each task, I was congratulated for the successful completion of that assignment, and just as I was to receive the gift, I suddenly woke from the dream. Wildly disappointed that I didn't stay asleep long enough to receive the gift, I leapt out of bed because I couldn't wait to write down the three concepts that were rattling around in my head: *Change...Confidence...Clarity.*

All I could see on the notepad in front of me were these three simple words, as I pondered what it meant. The next day, I asked a few friends to help me interpret this vivid dream. I couldn't understand how these three words could have translated into a "gift." Selfishly, I wanted to better understand the key to this amazing gift of freedom and life. To my friends, it was a simple translation. "Your very success to date, Jim, is due to those three gifts. You have the gift of *change*. Your ability to embrace change helped you deal with adversity and turn it into opportunity. Your gift of *confidence* allowed you to believe that anything is possible with a little diligence and hard work. Finally, your gift of *clarity* is what makes it all work. You can break down difficult problems into simple solutions and then communicate those solutions in a way that even a child could understand. Those are the things that make you a leader and have contributed to your personal and professional success."

This revelation floored me. They were right. Everything I have ever accomplished in life, from grammar school until my ascent to corporate leadership, came down to those three essential elements. Not only did I embrace these gifts, but I also began to teach them, and I've used them as a leadership guide for my employees, teammates, and friends. I have found these three keys especially relevant when encouraging students and helping them find their own path.

During this journey for students and with students, I developed a road map to self-determination and to freedom. I wanted to help others find their own path to academic, professional and even personal success. While building this road map, I became aware that my "gift" was only *what* to learn. I had to understand *how* to learn. When looking into my own learning journey, I realized that *how* to learn involved critical thinking, curiosity, and creativity. Those three critical success factors were enablers to help me continue on a path of lifelong learning. Next, I explored the question of *why* we learn. Recognizing that we are not alone in this world, I have outlined three elements that make up the *why*: collaboration because we live in a community both locally and globally, cultural literacy because understanding and adapting from other cultures can expand our own horizons, and character because that is the identity that will shape the way we interact with others.

Together they make up nine critical success factors, the very steps that enabled my journey to the C-Suite, the leadership roles in business. They also represent critical success factors that all leaders must learn to succeed. This "C-Suite Learning" is the heart of this book and a valuable road map to help you, the reader, form a path to your own learning journey. By practicing these 9 Cs, we can Live to Learn…freeing ourselves from personal and societal constraints to our freedom. Only then, will we truly Learn to Live.

C-Suite Learnings

What	Change	Confidence	Clarity
How	Critical Thinking	Curiosity	Creativity
Why	Collaboration	Cultural Literacy	Character

C-Suite Learnings includes:

What to Learn

1. **Change**: embracing change and growing from adversity.
2. **Confidence**: the inner strength that makes us believe in ourselves.
3. **Clarity**: making the complex simple through communication.

How to Learn

1. **Critical Thinking**: the algebra of thought.
2. **Curiosity**: discovering the joy of wonder.
3. **Creativity**: enabling our inner child; this is intelligence at play.

Why We Learn

1. **Collaboration**: leveraging the power of others working together.
2. **Cultural Literacy**: growing from the richness of diversity around us.
3. **Character**: establishing trust in ourselves and integrity among all.

This simple road map, while easy to outline, is more challenging to navigate. It requires a spark to ignite the determination and persistence we need to overcome our own mental obstacles that hold us back. We awaken that spark through awareness and a burning desire for freedom. Perhaps this book will be that spark!

Each of us wants to be free, yet few of us know how. Once you realize that freedom is not something given but rather something taken, you may then realize the responsibility you have for your own journey toward freedom. That journey begins with what you know. Many of us began our learning journey with Dr. Seuss, who reminded us with eloquence, "The more that you read, the more things you will know. The more that you learn, the more places you'll go."

While exploring this path to freedom, it is only natural to ask some basic questions. What makes an individual succeed or fail? What makes them happy or sad? What makes a person feel that they control their own destiny versus being held captive (physically or mentally) by others?

The goal of this work is to help you, the reader, find unfettered access to opportunity and happiness. Freedom is learning to rise above the challenges of daily life and learning to fly and, figuratively or even literally, to soar. You have all it takes to be free. Follow me, I will show you how.

FREEDOM TO LEARN IS FREEDOM TO EARN

Freedom is the real prize in life, the precious luxury item that often seems out of reach. It is the elusive dream of all humankind, there for the taking yet often elusive because it is hiding in plain view. Still, as my father tried to explain, there is a certain level of earning power needed to support even the most basic needs of life. While there is not a complete linear relationship between learning and earning power, there is clearly a correlation.

Those who have advanced degrees secure measurably stronger earning power, with college graduates earning, on average, more than 50 percent more than those with just a high school degree. According to a study by the Georgetown University Center on Education and the Workforce, the lifetime earnings of a college graduate are on average $1 million more than those of a high school graduate. Additionally, college graduates have a lower unemployment rate and are less likely to live in poverty. Of course, many other factors are involved, including choice of profession, field of study, and market conditions. Still, there is clearly a direct correlation between education and financial success. This is not to say that a formal education is the only path to success, it simply improves the odds.

The next chapter will outline some of the challenges with the state of education as we know it today. For some, the odds may seem insurmountable. The neighborhood may be hostile, the school system broken, and the deck stacked against your personal success. We must acknowledge those issues and, as a society, must work to improve the opportunity for everyone to have access to a quality education. This process, however, will be an evolution. The revolution must come from within each individual. Our ancestors had to study by candlelight with borrowed books. I used a set of encyclopedias, each volume coming free with a purchase from the grocery store. Through technology, we now have access to more information in the palm of our hands than anyone in the history of mankind. Let there be no excuse.

Education is Freedom hopes to inspire an awareness that your personal freedom is directly related to your knowledge; highlight already available technological resources that can enhance our learning; and provide a road map for each of us to take personal responsibility for our own self-determination. The education system may indeed be broken and the odds may seem stacked against you, but the freedom to learn is in your hands. Indeed, your own future and the future of humanity is in your hands.

CHAPTER 2

THE STATE OF EDUCATION: MAKING THE SYSTEM WORK FOR YOU

"The illiterate of the 21st century will not be those who cannot read and write, but those who cannot learn, unlearn, and relearn."

Alvin Toffler

If education is freedom, then clearly education is pivotal to the core of our democratic principles. A longstanding political science theory holds that a country's level of education attainment is a key factor in determining the emergence and sustainability of democratic political institutions. Despite its foundational role in a democratic society, many are challenging the delivery and even the importance of education. Democracy across the world is at risk. With the polarization of today's society, the foundational right to freedom of speech is also being challenged. Truth is under siege as misinformation and hostility have replaced critical thinking and civil discourse. Distrust and misinformation have also permeated our education systems. Fundamentally, ideology should not drive education.

With due respect to friends on both sides of the political spectrum, we are too often fighting about the wrong things. When it comes to political discourse about education, we are addressing the symptoms and not the cause. It isn't about teachers' unions with too much control, nor is it about school choice or fears of indoctrination. These are yesterday's issues, not tomorrow's. Instead, the challenge facing education is the need to completely reinvent our approach to teaching and learning to address the needs of the populace into the future. The system that we know today was overhauled at the dawn of the Industrial Age to teach a growing physical workforce. We now must reinvent education in a similar way to teach the thinkers and service providers of the Information Age.

Technologies at hand today and tomorrow will help facilitate this overhaul much in the same way the tools of yesterday helped us create our traditional classroom. We need to reinvent teaching and learning to make it more personal, more adaptable, and more scalable than ever before. The future of our community, our nation, and our world depends on our ability to improve the quality of education available to all of mankind.

Why is this important for the future of humanity? Our freedom of self-determination has a prerequisite: an *informed* electorate. If that electorate is armed with false information, incapable of critical thinking, or is influenced by outside forces then their actions and reactions can put democracy at risk. Today, more than ever, we must turn to the education, knowledge, and wisdom of each individual to discern right from wrong, truth from fiction, and success from failure. *Education Is Freedom* is, in this fashion, a handbook for humanity that allows us to individually and collectively understand the road map to freedom.

WHERE DOES HUMANITY GO TO SCHOOL?

Across the globe, education has expanded the knowledge base of the world, yet we still face a learning crisis both domestic and international. While many countries have significantly increased access to education, going to school isn't the same thing as learning. Worldwide, millions of children reach young adulthood without even the most basic skills, like proficient reading, calculating correct change from a sale, or understanding a transportation schedule.

In an age where young people are the fastest growing segment of the world's population, data from the UNESCO Institute for Statistics (UIS) reveals that an estimated 263 million children are out of school, overwhelmingly so in the least developed countries.[1] The International Commission on Financing Global Education Opportunity reported that a far larger number, 825 million young people worldwide, will not have basic literacy and numerical and digital knowledge to satisfy the jobs needed by the year 2030. Without some form of government or financial intervention, we face a serious risk of global instability and a constraint on worldwide economic growth.

Refugees and internally displaced people, now numbering over one hundred million, constitute another element of the global learning crisis. Two-thirds of these people are women and children. Host countries, many of which are fragile themselves, struggle to offer access to education for displaced immigrants. Even in America, we struggle to provide proper education to the millions of displaced children crossing our border every year.

Addressing today's massive global education crisis will require some disruption from the historical norms. Realistically, it will require the development of a new, more modern approach to aid delivery built on public-private partnership and a results-based financing model that rewards political and financial leadership. Since business is the ultimate source of demand for an educated workforce, there is also an important role for corporations to be more proactive in support for public education. Only through proactive intervention will we overcome obstacles to equitable access to learning. While showing improvement over the past few decades, equitable access must also address the realities of gender inequities. We still have a long way to go and much more work to do.

---

1 "263 Million Children and Youth Are Out of School," UNESCO UIS, July 15, 2016, http://uis.unesco.org/en/news/263-million-children-and-youth-are-out-school.

THE GENDER CHALLENGE

Today, more than 150 million girls around the world between the ages of six and seventeen are still not in school. To reap the full benefits of education, countries need to improve access and quality so that all girls can learn. Women with secondary education also have a better ability to make decisions in their household, including for their own health care. They are less likely to experience intimate partner violence, and they report higher levels of psychological well-being. They also have healthier children who are less likely to be malnourished and more likely to go to school and learn. Finally, better education for girls makes them more likely to participate fully in society and be active members of their community.

Despite making progress in gender parity, at today's pace it will take another century to reach true gender equality at the secondary school level in the least developed nations. Lack of education and related employment opportunities in these countries contributes to national, regional, and global security risks. Complicated by both ideological and financial challenges, countries need to improve access and quality so that all girls can learn.

These changes are especially crucial in some regions, such as Sub-Saharan Africa, where, on average, only 40 percent of girls complete lower secondary school. Countries also need policies to support healthy economic growth that will generate jobs for an expanding educated workforce. Among global education's most urgent challenges is a severe lack of trained teachers, particularly female instructors. An additional nine million trained teachers are needed in Sub-Saharan Africa by 2030. "When 130 million girls are unable to become engineers or journalists or CEOs because education is out of their reach, our world misses out on trillions of dollars that could strengthen the global economy, public health and stability," said Malala Yousafzai, Malala Fund co-founder and Nobel laureate. "If leaders are serious about building a better world, they need to start with serious investments in girls' secondary education."

I once had an opportunity to give the keynote address at a Texas Women's Foundation fundraiser. Speaking before a group of two thousand women at a luncheon was no small challenge. When I began, I could barely be heard above the din of plates clattering and women chatting. I told the story of a young Latina who was orphaned in Rio Grande, Texas, nearly ninety years before. She overcame impossible odds to get an education, earning two master's degrees and becoming a librarian for the local high school.

By the time I was halfway through the story, you could hear a pin drop as I spoke about her life. This remarkable woman put herself through school, raised six children, who grew up to include a doctor, a dentist, a noted philanthropist, a health care specialist, and a doctoral candidate. I closed the speech with a variation of the organization's motto: "Teach a woman, you help a family; help the family and you help the community; help the community and you help the world." I then introduced the woman, my mother-in-law, Angiolina Ramirez, to deafening applause!

Women, through education, will help us make this world a better place.

THE STATE OF AMERICAN EDUCATION

When researching the state of education for this book, I turned to friends up and down the education system, from teachers to superintendents; from school board members to college presidents; and from parents to students. The consistency of feedback, good and bad, was astounding. They told me: The system is broken, rigged, and/or biased. The system is underfunded and/or a waste of tax dollars. The system lacks accountability and is controlled by the teachers' unions. The system is accused of indoctrinating our children yet not teaching them. Some of this is political, some of it is perception and in some cases it is real. The noise in the system, unfortunately, is deafening making it harder for teachers to teach. Despite these horrific descriptions of the state of public education, there are wonderful examples of success stories where individuals have overcome the system, a school has accomplished a turnaround, or a district is embracing innovations with terrific results. Most teachers who I know teach with a passion for their craft. Sadly, too often they remain underpaid and underappreciated. Most school administrators I know are also committed to the success of their students.

Jonathan J. Sanford, president of the University of Dallas, notes that Plato said, "Any education is a matter of culture formation, for good or for ill intent." The Ancient Greek philosophers like Socrates, Plato, and Aristotle paid concerted attention to the political, social, and institutional influences of education. Sanford points out that Plato's credo in *The Laws* was that "you get education right, and culture flourishes; you get it wrong and culture falls ultimately into a tyranny of the mind and body. The link between education and culture," he says, "is inescapable, which is why so many of us are concerned about the distressing state of education in our country today. Whether fostered in the worst or the best of schools, the student is being formed one way or another and the shape given to his or her soul will prove of signature importance for the shape of our wider culture."[2] Most would agree that our education system badly needs attention. A host of issues face our public schools today, from the size of classrooms to the pervasive poverty levels in many parts of the country. Complicating the poverty challenge is an increase in single-family households, making childcare and supervision a legitimate obstacle. Meanwhile, we have seen an increase in social issues such as bullying, drugs, and violence. All these factors combine to create a more challenging learning environment. The obstacles can make education a privilege that is out of practical reach for too many.

These facts must be addressed:[3]

2 University of Dallas, Veritas Newsletter, January 2022.

3 Most of this data comes from the OECD report for 2022.

- The size of classrooms in many school systems has become unwieldy. A study by the National Center for Education Statistics found that 14 percent of US schools exceed capacity.
- In the US, more than 20 percent of our children live in poverty (defined as family incomes below $25,000), contributing to poor academic results and higher dropout rates.
- The high school graduation rate in the US is only 76 percent, ranking twenty-first among Organization for Economic Co-operation and Development (OECD) countries and falling well behind Portugal, Slovenia, Finland, and Japan, which are all above 95 percent.
- US high school graduates are often unprepared for college. Nearly forty percent of all students entering college need remedial courses.
- In the US, nearly 50 percent of students who start college never complete a post-secondary degree, putting us outside of the top ten industrialized nations in college graduation rates.

How do American students compare with their peers around the world? The Pew Research Center recently reported data from international math and science assessments that indicate US students have fallen behind many other advanced industrial nations. One of the biggest cross-national tests is the Programme for International Student Assessment (PISA). The most recent PISA results placed the US at thirty-eighth of seventy-one countries in math and twenty-fourth in science. These should be alarming statistics for a country that hopes to maintain leadership on the world stage. Other industrialized countries are simply performing better than the US on the fundamentals of education.

The Brookings Institution identified another issue in 2021 that they defined as the "male college crisis." The worldwide gender gap identified earlier for women is going the wrong direction for males in post-secondary education. While women have outpaced men in college enrollment and completion rates for decades, this disparity has become worse since the pandemic. In the fall of 2021, men represented only four in ten college students.[4] This problem has been worsening for those who are already low income and disadvantaged.

Does all this matter? Should we be concerned about America falling behind other countries in high school or college graduation rates? Is it worth the societal investment in public education?

I think we can all agree that it *does* matter and that societal investment in public education is essential for the continued growth in prosperity of any country. Some would argue that our investment is already high and that we are not receiving the commensurate results. Blaming the system or pulling our children out of schools is not the solution. Just as an individual or a corporation goes through a life cycle and sometimes needs to be reinvented, so must our education system. This will not happen overnight, but we must remain focused on the importance of this initiative to society because the cost of inaction is high.

SOCIETAL COST OF INADEQUATE EDUCATION

America loses hundreds of billions of dollars each year when young people fail to graduate from high school. These costs include lost productivity, which leads to lower tax revenues. Meanwhile, taxpayers' costs are increased, resulting in higher costs in health care, public assistance, and criminal justice systems. Any nation, without a solution, faces reduced global economic competitiveness. A symposium

4 Richard V. Reeves and Ember Smith, "The Male College Crisis Is Not Just in Enrollment, But Completion," The Brookings Institution, October 8, 2021, https://www.brookings.edu/articles/the-male-college-crisis-is-not-just-in-enrollment-but-completion/.

at Teachers College, Columbia University highlighted "The Social Costs of Inadequate Education." Some of their findings include:

- A high school dropout earns about $260,000 less over a lifetime than a high school graduate and more than $1 million less over a lifetime than a college graduate.
- High school dropouts have a life expectancy that is 9.2 years shorter than high school graduates.
- America could save between $7.9 billion and $10.8 billion annually by improving educational attainment among all recipients of temporary assistance for food and housing.
- A one-year increase in average years of schooling for dropouts would reduce murder and assault by almost 30 percent, motor vehicle theft by 20 percent, arson by 13 percent, and burglary and larceny by about 6 percent.
- College graduates are three times more likely to vote than Americans without a high school degree.

If the societal cost of inadequate education is so high, then we should all agree that it must be fixed. The problem has been "how" to address the challenges with our education system. First, we should explore some of the root causes behind the shortcomings. We can then look to reasons for hope...and there are many.

UNDERSTANDING THE ROOT CAUSES

Despite today's challenges, we have made significant progress with education at a global and domestic level. At the turn of the twentieth century, less than 10 percent of the US population had a high school diploma and less than 2 percent graduated from college. The vast majority of those educated in 1900 were white males. Those were, indeed, different times that required a different objective for education in the US and many other places worldwide. The Industrial Revolution caused a need for standardization and a demand for an educated workforce.

John D. Rockefeller founded the General Education Board, which published a 1912 report describing the role of public education in satisfying the need for an educated workforce. The report outlined the importance of training students for the workforce, badly needed in the industrial economy of the times. This began a movement in education to standardize teaching and measurement around a norm, or an average. Schools around the country began to adopt the Gary Plan, named after the industrialized city of Gary, Indiana, where students were divided into groups by age and rotated through different classes for standardized periods of time. School bells were introduced to mirror factory bells, and standardized testing was introduced to measure individuals against a "norm."

This was not some maniacal scheme to stamp out individualism. It was a practical solution to the need for an educated workforce. It was also an acknowledgment of the teaching challenges in an urbanized population, where some level of standardization and conformity was needed. As a nation, we went from personalized teaching in the little red schoolhouse to mass production of students through elementary and high school. Through necessity, standardized measurement, curriculums, and testing became the norm.

One of the most frequent criticisms of standardized testing is the inability to measure creativity and critical thinking as it relates to problem solving. This isn't a new debate. It goes back to the origins of modern standardized testing that can be traced back to French psychologist Alfred Binet. In 1905, he began developing a standardized test of intelligence that became known as the Stanford-Binet Intelligence Test, the first known measurement of IQ as we think of it today. The US began testing for aptitude in WWI to group soldiers according to their mental abilities.

At first, such standardized testing seemed to be a blessing. The military could benefit by finding the soldiers with officer potential. Children could be assessed and grouped with other students and curriculums designed for their respective mental abilities. Meanwhile, psychologists like Alfred Binet of France and Lewis Terman of the United States continued to study the measurement of the way individuals think. In 1926, the first Scholastic Aptitude Tests (SAT) were launched by the College Board, a nonprofit group of universities and other educational organizations. Beginning in 1934, Harvard adopted the SAT for admission and scholarship recipients and the testing became widely used thereafter.[5]

Many believe that such testing may have long-term implications for schools, providing advantages or disadvantages by community. Some critics believe that cultural and language bias in historical testing models could disadvantage gender, racial, and economically marginalized populations. The downside of such standardization is that it doesn't recognize that people learn in very different ways. Those who could conform and adapt to the "standard" would excel. Often, those who didn't became dropouts or, in some cases, were relegated to "special" education classes where someone with a learning disability like dyslexia may have been lumped in with others with severe mental handicaps.

Todd Rose, a high school dropout who eventually became a Harvard professor, addresses these challenges in his book, *The End of Average*. Rose highlights the work of University of California, Santa Barbara neuroscientist Michael Miller, who found that "not only was each person's brain different from the average, they were all different from one another." In his work, Rose offers a blueprint for establishing an education system that is consistent with the principles of individuality and that will address the learning needs of *all* students

5 "History of Standardized Testing in the United States," National Education Association, June 25, 2020, https://www.nea.org/professional-excellence/student-engagement/tools-tips/history-standardized-testing-united-states.

not just the average students. He advances the idea that education should grant credentials not diplomas; replace grades with competency; and let students determine their own educational pathway. While it may be a radical idea, finding ways to curate old and new learning systems to benefit the enhancement of personal education is likely the long-term solution.

Our society and its needs have changed. We've moved from the Industrial Age to the Information Age, yet our education system has not yet kept up with these changes.

Today's educated workforce needs a very different kind of education, yet the system is unlikely to respond quickly enough to address these needs in the future. Very simply, our education system and even the fundamental methods of teaching and learning have not kept pace with the necessary changes of today's society. Change is hard...and change is slow.

REASONS FOR HOPE

In the Information Age, our educational needs will differ but so will the ways of providing that education. New technologies—like Artificial Intelligence and more affordable, connected learning devices—are already changing the way we teach and learn as we will explore in depth in a later chapter.

Meanwhile, philanthropy in America is stronger than ever. Total US charitable donations reached nearly $485 billion in 2021, a 4 percent increase from 2020. Perhaps the most telltale sign of change is that corporations, which have one of the greatest influences on elevating underserved communities, increased giving by 23.8 percent. Individual donors are following suit. Warren Buffett has promised to donate more than 99 percent of his wealth. To date, he has given more than $50 billion. In 2010, he, Bill Gates, and Melinda French Gates launched the Giving Pledge, asking billionaires to donate at least half of their wealth to charitable organizations. Since that time, they have grown this list to over 230 individuals in more than twenty-eight countries.

Much of this money is going toward education initiatives. More individuals, foundations, and corporations are committed to transforming the education system in America to provide greater access to quality education. The business community is also responding, recognizing that an educated community is essential for the quality of workers as well as the quality of life in the communities where we live and work. Murphy Oil and Murphy USA funded such a program in their hometown, El Dorado, Arkansas. The corporation provides 100% of the funds for the El Dorado Promise, providing scholarships for any accredited Arkansas public university or community college. More corporations see a commitment to education as an investment rather than as a charitable contribution. It is possible for them to measure a return on investment on dollars spent in the community to improve the quality of the available workforce, and quality of life in our society.

Another indication of progress is the increasing commitment to providing free or low-cost access to education through our community college network. Many communities have funded a "promise" to allow any student deciding to attend a community college to do so at no cost. Dallas, Texas, recently implemented an appropriately named "Dallas County Promise" to provide the cost of tuition at any of the seven campuses at Dallas College or a last-dollar tuition grant at partnering colleges and universities. While private college tuitions continue to increase, at least students have access to a springboard from which they can move forward. Many of these students complete two years at the community college, excel in their respective programs, then move on to complete the final two years of their education at a private institution. Meanwhile, "early college" programs are increasingly providing high school students with an opportunity to take college courses that give them a head start or even the ability to complete an associate degree while still in high school.

Measurement and sharing of data will go a long way toward improvement of the system. Todd Williams, a retired partner and managing director of Goldman Sachs, committed his post-banking future to the transformation of public education. He is the founding Chairman and CEO of an organization called The Commit Partnership, the nation's largest educational collective impact organization. It has partnered with more than two hundred institutions, including fifteen school districts and eight higher-education institutions. The organization is focused on using data to identify and expand on the best practices across the system. Through measurement and replication of successful programs, it has already demonstrated an ability to achieve dramatic improvement in public school effectiveness.

Reducing class size, expanding of charter schools, and school choice programs are a few of the many ways being explored to facilitate near-term improvement in the public education arena. None of these programs by themselves will create the systemic change needed for the long-term transformation of our education system. These challenges are unlikely to be solved through government alone. If the business community represents the single largest source of "demand" for an educated workforce, then can the business community play a greater role in this transformation?

ROLE OF BUSINESS IN EDUCATIONAL TRANSFORMATION

For generations, many businesses have been sitting on the sidelines of public education while government on the local, state, and national level has struggled to keep pace with students' changing needs. From a business perspective, this is a question of supply and demand. The greatest demand for an educated workforce comes from business. As a chief executive, I learned over the years that the ultimate success of most corporations will depend on the quality of their workforce. I found that the supply of quality workforce was lacking. Business has an insatiable appetite for skilled and educated employees. Why then shouldn't it take a proactive role in the development of those future employees?

This was the model that inspired creation of the Education is Freedom Foundation, a 501(c)(3) nonprofit organization dedicated to providing opportunities for all students to succeed. As business leaders, government officials, and entrepreneurs, the foundation's board was and is committed to creating an educated workforce that can build effective companies and strong communities in today's knowledge-based economy. The original purpose: to bring together corporations in order to tackle our communal need for quality employees by building a bridge between public school children and future jobs. Since then, school systems have embraced the need of advisory services, resulting in a collaborative effort to help students achieve their full potential with the support of public and private funding.

The concept is simply to provide students with the inspiration and confidence to learn, offer college and career guidance along their educational journey. By putting advisory counselors in public high schools, we could intercept students at an early age and give them the confidence, tools, road map, and sometimes even the scholarship support to pursue a higher education. Even if they choose not to go on to college, we aim to help them complete high school and be better prepared for the workforce.

Those involved in the Education is Freedom Foundation soon realize that their investment is not a normal philanthropic gift. Instead, they enjoy a measurable return on investment by gaining access to quality future employees. The collaboration between business and local government produced a program called the *Mayor's Internship*, or *Dallas Works* within Dallas. With the mayor's strong voice in the community, corporations have been encouraged to hire Dallas ISD students for summer internships. The Education is

Freedom Foundation facilitates the program, selecting the students and training them for the opportunities ahead.

The students gain exposure to corporations through internships that provide an understanding of the professional world that is beyond most students' imaginations. Corporations such as 7-Eleven, J.P. Morgan, PepsiCo, and many more have learned the benefits of bringing interns into the fold and inspiring them to become future employees. The students' lives are often changed beyond anyone's expectation. Imagine a young person from a humble background showing up for work, riding an elevator for the first time, and learning firsthand about what happens within the walls of those tall towers downtown.

Adan Gonzalez was a product of this effort. He grew up in a large Mexican-American family in South Dallas. His parents were hardworking laborers doing a wide range of janitorial and service jobs to help feed their large family. Neither had gone to college, so neither could provide advice or guidance on the educational front. In fact, the communal assumption was that each young person would secure a job as soon as practically possible to help the family survive.

Adan seemed to have been likely to follow that same path. He was a tough kid, a fighter by stature and personality. Because of that, he was a prime target for a gang. However, he had different plans in mind. He found the Education is Freedom program, or perhaps, as fate would have it, we found him. He joined the cause, and instead of fighting on the streets, he fought to learn and succeed.

It wasn't an easy path for Adan. He embraced the coaching and advice of his Education is Freedom counselor, but when his first internship opportunity, a job with Bank of America, was presented to him, Adan declined. Instead, he chose to work at a local warehouse where he could earn $1 more per hour. Today, he laughs at his own immaturity. "I had no idea what went on inside those corporate walls and thought it was all about making more money now...not later," he said. The next summer, he took advantage of the internship opportunity offered him, working for an advertising firm in a role that opened his eyes to greater work possibilities. "I was no longer an outsider," he said. "I was accepted by the people at the agency as one of them, a contributing member of the team. This gave me the confidence in myself and made me realize, *Yes, I can.* I can do this or any other job that comes my way as long as I continue to learn and prepare for the opportunity."

I first met Adan when he was speaking from the podium at a Black-tie gala for Junior Achievement (JA). Speaking as the JA Student of the Year, he acknowledged Junior Achievement's importance in helping him succeed, but he also highlighted his experience with the Education is Freedom Foundation in helping him navigate through high school. He announced his acceptance to Georgetown University for the fall. I made my way through the crowd to congratulate Adan, finding him to be grateful for his transformation after discovering that education is indeed freedom. Adan went on to Georgetown, became an intercollegiate boxing champion, and graduated with honors.

Most gratifying was his return to Dallas, where he would teach grammar school in his old neighborhood, inspiring others to learn. While there, he created his own foundation, The Puede Network, which translates roughly into the "Yes I Can" Network. His life's work is to inspire his siblings and neighbors to help themselves to the American dream. Adan has since gone back to school, earning graduate degrees in education at Harvard and Columbia University. He was recently named a White House Fellow and is working on education initiatives in Washington, DC. Helping this young man achieve the American dream is a gift that will keep on giving for generations to come. Adan is not yet famous, but he certainly will be one day. He is not wealthy, but wealth does not motivate him...freedom motivates him. As he will tell you, education *is* his freedom. Adan is one of hundreds of thousands of young people whose lives have been transformed by the collaborative efforts of the business community.

Some corporations have long realized the importance and benefit of supporting education. Texas Instruments, Microsoft, AT&T, JP Morgan, and many more have contributed billions toward educational initiatives, but the opportunity is so much greater. If all corporations could better understand the return on investment possible through STEAM (science, technology engineering, arts, and math), we could invest in modern technologies that will help transform the learning experience. If all corporations provided internship opportunities, we could expose more youth to the vocational or higher education opportunities required to fill their future jobs. As knowledge-based jobs increase in importance, corporations must step up and play a proactive role in educating their future. The Education is Freedom Foundation is one of thousands of portals for corporations, foundations or individuals to invest in the education of our future generations. Ultimately, the success of these programs will come down to the individual student, inspiring learning one individual at a time.

THE ROLE OF THE INDIVIDUAL IN EDUCATION

With the many challenges confronting public education today, many simply give up. We've all heard their reasons:

> "I can't afford school."
> "The man is keeping me down."
> "My teachers are incompetent."
> "The dog ate my homework."

You name it. The excuses are many and sometimes very real. Urban America has been struggling for years, and public education has not been the requisite antidote for poverty. If the system is so badly broken, then what do we do? Is there hope for the individual to succeed despite the many challenges? As we contemplate these challenges, we must acknowledge that persevering in education is not about waiting for miracle solutions. Yes, many promising innovations are on the horizon, but it will take generations to transform the system. Incremental improvements must be embraced and replicated. Meanwhile, finding the path to success means making productive use of the tools available while avoiding the mistakes of the past. We must acknowledge the many forces pushing against fundamentally improved education systems around the world, but as individuals we must also never give up.

In the near term, the power is in the individual. That's where we should all find hope. So many success stories are to be discovered. It has been repeatedly demonstrated that an individual, armed with desire and a belief that they can succeed, will overcome even the most dysfunctional school system or the most challenging environment. The "system" will take years, decades, or even centuries to transform. The individual, with an understanding of the importance of self-reliance, a strong degree of determination, and a little guidance, can overcome immeasurable odds to succeed. The objective of this book, *Education Is Freedom,* is to provide a road map for that journey and the inspiration for one's individual success. Individual determination and thirst for knowledge are the keys to unlocking the American dream.

The student will face decisions regarding the time, effort, and investment to gain the desired degree of learning. Because of the spiraling cost of education, many have questioned the value and suggest there may not be a reasonable return on investment. Is it worth the personal investment for an individual to attend college?

Going to college, seeking vocational training, or choosing to become an entrepreneur are all very personal decisions. Whenever speaking with young people contemplating one of those paths, I often break it down into the following advice. First, I advise them to pursue what they enjoy. Whether serving as a plumber or a brain surgeon, the successful individual must strive to have a career that they love. Otherwise, their work will become tedious despite the potential remuneration. Whichever path they choose, continued learning is fundamental to their success.

Second, I advise them to consider the odds of success in achieving any career goal. Some point to Michael Dell or Steve Jobs, both of whom dropped out of school to build billion-dollar enterprises. In the same fashion, LeBron James didn't attend college but beat the odds to make professional basketball a career. To be sure, these individuals were highly successful but also were the anomalies. With advanced educational degrees, the probability of success is simply higher for most people. Even if one can be successful without the degree, we still need continued learning to successfully manage our lives.

The third piece of advice I offer is to give yourself a chance. Most of us have no idea what we want to be when we are in high school. We simply haven't seen enough of the world or explored enough of our options to know what is possible. College, in many cases, provides the time and broadens the awareness necessary for a young person to make informed choices about the rest of their life. Yes, the cost of college can be an obstacle, but it should never become an excuse. The community college network or availability of state-funded universities can significantly reduce the cost while providing the additional runway that young people often need to determine their true passion. Additionally, the true "cost" of college is often less than it would appear on the surface. We must avoid being intimidated by the "sticker price" because of the increasing availability of scholarship support. Many of the most expensive schools have "discount" rates of as much as 40–50 percent representing the scholarship support provided. My advice to all students is give yourself a chance. Aim for the stars and, if you miss, you'll still hit the moon. My high school guidance counselor advised me to attend a local community college because he knew that I couldn't afford a four-year school. In reality, my chances of a full scholarship at an Ivy

League school were far better than my chances of financial support from the local community college. This is why I encourage young people to strive for the best with confidence that the fallback options will always be available.

Many vocations do not require a college degree yet provide significant economic reward and personal gratification. Becoming a builder, a plumber, a welder, or even a pilot are all essential roles in our society. While none of those jobs require a college degree, we sometimes forget that they too require a high degree of education and hands-on training. Whether pursuing a trade or seeking a secondary or even tertiary degree, the most important consideration is that we *do not quit*. Stay the course and keep learning.

So where *did* humanity go to school throughout the ages? Many of the famous Greek philosophers came from wealthy families and attended schools like the Lyceum, but Socrates was from a poor family. It didn't stop him. His insatiable appetite for knowledge led him to read and to pursue self-study. Some of the greatest minds in science like Isaac Newton and Charles Darwin were self-educated. We've all heard the stories of Abraham Lincoln studying voraciously by candlelight with borrowed textbooks. Today, each of us has access to more information through our cellphone or via the internet than any human has enjoyed since the dawn of time. It is time for each of us to put those tools to work, harnessing the power of knowledge to unlock our freedom; to unlock the American dream.

CHAPTER 3

LIVING THE DREAM: UNLOCKING YOUR FUTURE

"In America, with education and hard work, it really does not matter where you came from; it matters only where you are going."

Condoleezza Rice

No doubt, the concept of the American dream is a crucial part of the ethos of American culture. Since the birth of our country, it has been the beacon of hope for immigrants near and far, providing equal opportunity for those willing to take a chance, work hard, and choose to take control of their own destiny. James Truslow Adams, in his 1931 book *The Epic of America,* first introduced the phrase "American dream." During the darkest hours of the Depression, he provided hope for America, saying, "It is not a dream of motor cars and high wages merely, but a dream of social order in which each man and each woman shall be able to attain to the fullest stature of which they are innately capable, and be recognized by others for what they are, regardless of the fortuitous circumstances of birth or position."[6] It is clearly a unique proposition, providing hope that nearly anyone, even those of humble beginnings, can take advantage of education, knowledge, and persistence

6 Thomas W. Adams, *The Epic of America* (New York, NY: Blue Ribbon Books, 1931).

to accomplish anything. Neither education, nor freedom, nor the American dream are free; but if the currency is hard work and determination, then each of us has the resources needed for success.

This grand idea of a personal dream of success shared by all is thought to be uniquely American. Dr. Ben Carson, during a speech to the Circle Ten Chapter of the Boy Scouts of America, reflected that "there is no Chinese dream, Russian dream, or even Canadian dream…only the American dream." That's simple yet powerful stuff, and there is a reason behind it. We are indeed a unique group of people, a true melting pot of the world. Together, our collective insight curates a remarkable experience for us all, with our democracy and democratic beliefs leading the way.

That opportunity may not always be equal, nor fair, nor just. But that doesn't mean the opportunity does not exist. The price may be higher for some, the hill bigger to climb and the obstacles more intimidating, but the opportunity remains omnipresent for anyone willing to make the personal investment in time and effort. We all have access to the American dream. Even those on the other side of the world.

The Chinese have adopted an important, but often overlooked, principle of the American dream. In some ways, it is one that we, as Americans, have sometimes forgotten. That principle is one of *individual* self-improvement. In the *New York Times,* American journalist Thomas Friedman wrote an opinion piece entitled, "China Needs Its Own Dream" that led him to being credited with popularizing the concept in China. In 2013, China's new paramount leader, Xi Jinping, began promoting the Chinese Dream, leading to its widespread use in the Chinese media. Friedman notes that he only deserves partial credit for the concept being adopted in China. "The concept of 'China Dream,'" he says, "was created by my friend Peggy Liu, as the motto for her NGO about how to introduce Chinese to the concept of sustainability." Journalists and government officials now use this phrase to describe the importance of individual self-improvement in Chinese society.[7]

The idea of individual self-improvement is paramount to the American dream as practiced by anyone, anywhere in the world. That is why we tie this dream to education and knowledge. No one will *give* us the American dream. No one will serve us personal freedom on a platter. Rather, it comes from within. It comes through self-improvement. It comes through knowledge, education, and continued learning. The Chinese may never adopt the true principles of the American dream, but they have focused on self-improvement, its most critical element.

A desire to protect this right to self-improvement led our founding fathers to include the building blocks of the American dream in our Declaration of Independence in that "all men are created equal" and maintain the right to "Life, Liberty and the pursuit of Happiness." In a letter to George Wythe, another of our founding fathers, Thomas Jefferson said, "I think by far the most important bill in our whole code is that for the diffusion of knowledge among the people. No other sure foundation can be devised for the preservation of freedom and happiness."[8]

WHO LIVES THE AMERICAN DREAM?

So who is it that actually "lives" the American dream? Let's explore some examples of those who embody the principles and live the American dream, as they are everywhere around us. Let's start with one of the richest men in the world, Warren Buffett, whose wealth is estimated to be more than $100 billion. He is thought to be among the top ten wealthiest individuals in the entire world. Buffett was

7 Thomas L. Friedman, "Opinion: China Needs Its Own Dream," *New York Times,* October 2, 2012, https://www.nytimes.com/2012/10/03/opinion/friedman-china-needs-its-own-dream.html.

8 "Founders Online: From Thomas Jefferson to George Wythe, 13 August 1786," National Archives and Records Administration, accessed July 20, 2023, https://founders.archives.gov/documents/Jefferson/01-10-02-0162.

born in Omaha, Nebraska, in 1930, the second of three children to Leila and Congressman Howard Buffett. In 1942, his father was elected to the first of several terms in the House of Representatives, moving his family to Washington, DC, where Warren attended high school. His senior yearbook picture says, "likes math…a future stockbroker."

Buffett was born into neither poverty nor wealth. Instead, he found his passion and pursued it with determination and persistence. He displayed an interest in business and investing at an early age, inspired by a book he borrowed from the Omaha Public Library at age seven, *One Thousand Ways to Make $1000*. He began to pursue some of those ways: selling chewing gum door to door, delivering newspapers, selling golf balls, and detailing cars, among other ventures. On his first income tax return in 1944, it is said that Buffett took a $35 deduction for the use of his bicycle and watch on his paper route.

Buffett's interest in the stock market and investing dated back to childhood days he spent in his father's brokerage office. His father took interest in educating the young Buffett, at one point taking him to visit the New York Stock Exchange when he was ten. At eleven, Buffett bought three shares of Cities Service Preferred, his first venture in stock acquisition. In 1947, Buffett entered the Wharton School of the University of Pennsylvania, later transferring to the University of Nebraska, where he graduated with a bachelor of science in business administration. After Harvard Business School rejected him, he enrolled in Columbia Business School, earning an MA in economics in 1951. While at Columbia, he became a protege of Benjamin Graham, widely known as the "father of value investing."

So, if the American dream isn't about wealth, then why did I use Buffett's story as a personification of the American dream? That is a fair question. The answer is because Buffett cares very little about personal wealth, in its traditional sense. Rather, he recognizes that his fortune gives him the most valuable thing in the world: freedom.

Buffett enjoys the freedom to learn (he has estimated that he spends 80 percent of his day reading); freedom to earn (he has built his own financial empire, his way); freedom to live (his humble lifestyle is legendary; he has resided in the same simple frame home, purchased for about $31,000, since 1958); and freedom to give (his generosity has shaped the future of American philanthropy).

Buffett didn't become one of the world's wealthiest men through inheritance. Instead, he found his passion: value investing. He then became obsessed with acquiring knowledge of that business practice. After learning the principles and graduating with a master's degree, he didn't stop learning. In fact, his learning was just beginning. Buffett became the Oracle of Omaha, creating Berkshire Hathaway and becoming one of the world's most successful investors...through knowledge. When he was asked about the key to his success, he pointed to a stack of books. "Read five hundred pages like this every day," he said. "That's how knowledge works. It builds up, like compound interest."

Yes, Buffett is a living example of the American dream, but many misinterpret his end game as aiming to be one of the richest men in the world. To Buffett, wealth is simply a byproduct of success. His wealth never changed his lifestyle. The lifestyle of a billionaire will evoke visions of mansions, jewelry, vacation homes, and expensive cars. That's never been the case for Buffett. He doesn't live the lifestyle of the rich and famous because his American dream and his personal freedom aren't about wealth; they are about having freedom to do the things he wants to do, when, where, and how he wishes to do them.

The American dream is not a dream of merely material plenty. It is the dream of one's ability to grow to one's fullest development undeterred by the barriers or social order restrictions of other civilizations. It is a dream shared by many from around the world who sometimes overcome incredible odds to seek the opportunity that America has to offer.

Indra Nooyi, former chair and CEO of PepsiCo, is another living example of the American dream, but she was born into very different circumstances than Warren Buffett.

Growing up in India, she lived in a communal house with her parents and grandparents. Her grandfather would wake her up at dawn and feign poor vision, asking young Indra to read to him. This was his way of encouraging her to read.

Education became Nooyi's path to freedom. Growing up in Madras, her family expected she wed by the young age of nineteen and immediately start to build a family. When her sister enrolled in school, her mother went on a fast, threatening to starve herself to death unless she dropped out. Her mom thankfully gave up after a few days. Nooyi's dedication to her studies landed her an opportunity to attend Yale School of Management. In 1994, she began her career and ended up at PepsiCo, rising through the ranks over the years by demonstrating her dedication, hard work, and profound knowledge of the business. She became the CEO in 2006 and was named chairman of PepsiCo in 2007, leading the giant beverage company to success over the next twelve years.

By most measures and certainly the standards of her family back in India, Nooyi is wealthy. But her American dream and her personal freedom do not come from her wealth alone. Instead, her freedom stems from her knowledge, which empowers Nooyi to pursue whatever path her heart desires. She is yet another example of how the American dream is not a race to accumulate wealth but rather a journey to find freedom.

Immigration of all kinds is fueled by the American dream. When we think of immigrants, we often have an "image" in mind, but the American dream represents a beacon of hope for people of every race and religion from all over the world. Bob and Myrna Schlegel grew up in a small Mennonite community outside of Toronto, Canada. As with so many immigrants, they heard the American dream call to them from across the border. Despite their humble roots, they were equipped with a strong education—Bob with a degree in accounting and Myrna as a registered nurse. They packed their car and drove their young family to Dallas, Texas, to build a better life.

Myrna used her healthcare education to start a nursing home that quickly grew to become a chain of nursing homes. Bob began a business called Pavestone, selling paving stone materials to contractors and individuals, even reaching retail customers through Home Depot. Myrna eventually sold her chain of nursing homes and helped fund the expansion of her husband's successful paving stone business. These two young Canadians who came to America with little more than their strong faith in God and a persistent determination to succeed were able to build a highly successful enterprise. They represent one example of millions of stories of immigrants who came to America to find success; but what they *did* with that success is a common theme among so many immigrant families.

The first thing they did with their wealth was to educate their children. As with so many immigrant families who discovered the American dream, they realized the importance of education and passed that priority along to their children. The second commonality is their philanthropic hearts. My dear friend Bob Schlegel, often quotes his favorite passage from the Bible: "to whom much is given… much will be required" Luke 12:48 (NKJV). The Schlegel family's heart and their commitment to paying it forward says it all.

The American dream, powered by education, has become the great equalizer in American life. It provides for opportunity, regardless of race, religion, or socioeconomic background. It propelled this nation of immigrants to become one of the wealthiest in the world, but it has not always been an easy path and the dream has not always been available to all.

UNDERSTANDING THE BARRIERS TO THE DREAM

In his "Letter from Birmingham Jail" (1963), Martin Luther King pointed out that the civil rights movement was about African Americans' quest for the American dream: "We will win our freedom because the sacred heritage of our nation and the eternal will of God are embodied in our echoing demand. When these disinherited children of God sat down at lunch counters they were in reality standing up for what is best in the American dream and for the most sacred values in our Judeo-Christian heritage, thereby bringing our nation back to those great wells of democracy which were dug deep by the founding fathers in their formulation of the Constitution and the Declaration of Independence."

Considering the social unrest today and through recent history, one could argue that the American dream is no longer relevant or even reachable for some. Michael Hout, professor of Sociology at New York University, completed a study that said: "Your circumstances at birth—specifically, what your parents do for a living—are an even bigger factor in how far you get in life than we had previously realized. Generations of Americans considered the United States to be a land of opportunity. This research raises some sobering questions about that image."[9]

Our country's very foundation of equal opportunity is also under pressure. A simple look at the disparity of wealth in this country would indicate that the problem is real. For example, the Federal Reserve states what many of us are aware of: "In the United States, the average Black and Hispanic or Latino households earn about half as much as the average White household and own only about 15 to 20 percent as much net wealth. This wealth gap has widened notably over the past few decades. At the same time, overall wealth

---

9 "The American Dream Is Even Harder to Achieve than We Thought," MarketWatch, September 5, 2018, https://www.marketwatch.com/story/the-american-dream-iseven-harder-to-achieve-than-we-thought-2018-09-04.

inequality has also grown."[10] If we are in one of those disadvantaged families, do we allow this to become an excuse, or do we turn it into opportunity?

So much of one's opportunity comes down to the way we see ourselves. Stedman Graham is a successful author, businessman, leader, and a close friend. He is also a powerfully inspirational force in education. Graham embodies the spirit that can lead to an individual's success. In his book *Identity: Your Passport to Success*, he speaks about his own journey of self-discovery. "I was a young 6-foot-6 black guy. What did everyone say I was? A basketball player. So, I was that," he said, "I lived the label."

He said he was angry at the system and had to hold in his fear, feeling like a victim in his own right. Then one day, he said he had an awakening. "It wasn't about race," he said, "it was about me not knowing who I was and not having a process for becoming successful. I'd been told it was about race, but I suddenly realized that somebody had fed me a bill of goods, and I had bought into it. If I'd bought into the notion that it was about race, there was no way out—I would be trying to solve what the problem wasn't." Stedman makes a powerful statement about self-determination. I have had the pleasure of sitting in an audience, hearing Graham deliver his message of identity to an auditorium full of inner-city students of many ethnicities. I've heard him tell them that their identity is theirs to form and to warn them about others trying to apply labels to them. From the wide eyes and nodding heads in the audience, it was clear that they too felt that life was acting upon them instead of feeling like they were in control. Graham emphasizes that *this* is the value of education—to let anyone, anywhere, anytime establish their own identity through learning to become the person they want to be, not the person they are told they are.

---

10 "Survey of Consumer Finances (SCF)," Board of Governors of the Federal Reserve System, December 9, 2019, https://www.federalreserve.gov/econres/scfindex.htm.

Despite circumstances and recent trends, many like Stedman Graham power through difficulties and still become shining examples of the American dream. While there are numerous ways to accomplish this, education is the common denominator and the most foundational of options. It is internal in nature, meaning you don't have to rely upon others to gain knowledge. Our own personal initiative to gain knowledge is, in some ways, the most powerful antidote for poverty. While many collective efforts will help bridge the gap that has widened over the years, education remains at the top of this list.

From this perspective, the American dream is not dead. It is very much alive but sometimes hidden under a societal construct that requires us to dig deeper and remain dedicated to our goal: opportunity. The beauty of the American dream and the wonder of the American miracle is that since our country's inception, it has been resilient and able to self-correct to constantly improve. Sure, we still have a lot of work to do together. But there is hope. If there wasn't, how could a young man or woman from an underserved and impoverished community become president of the United States or start a successful investment firm? These aren't one-offs anymore, but our work is not done. It is just beginning.

HORATIO ALGER AND A REASON FOR HOPE

While some may claim the American Dream is no longer possible, my story and the story of so many others will show reason for hope that the dream is still very much alive. To find evidence of this hope, let me introduce you to an organization called the Horatio Alger Association of Distinguished Americans. Many of the individuals whose stories are highlighted in this work are members of the Horatio Alger Association. Dr. Kenneth Beebe, along with Dr. Norman Vincent Peale founded the organization in 1947 to honor the achievements of outstanding Americans who succeeded despite adversity. He named the association after Horatio Alger, a nineteenth-century author of hundreds of "rags-to-riches" stories emphasizing the importance of perseverance and hard work to overcome adversity.

The association has been highly successful in its mission to change the lives of students facing adversity by providing scholarships, mentorship, and support to deserving young people. Each year they bring together hundreds of young scholars to meet and learn from successful past honorees. I was nominated by a dear friend, Lou Brock, Hall of Fame Baseball player, who invited me to his own induction in 2002. I was very fortunate to be inducted into the Association in 2005, side by side with my friend and childhood hero, Buzz Aldrin.

Each year, I attend an annual gathering in Washington D.C. and have the privilege of meeting fellow honorees and a new crop of scholarship recipients. After each meeting, I am more humbled by these young students and their strength in overcoming adversity that bears little resemblance to my own. Hearing stories of today's challenges such as homelessness, addiction, incarceration, or abuse makes the challenges of poverty alone seem like a cakewalk. Yes, the challenges facing our young people today may be greater and more severe than ever before. Still, the spirit of determination of those individuals is palpable.

Once we help to show them the path, many have proven their ability to overcome impossible odds to prevail. The system for many is broken. The hand that many of us are dealt by circumstance of birth or environment can be overwhelming, but hope will always prevail if one can be shown the way. Throughout this book I will share examples and anecdotes of Horatio Alger members like Indra Nooyi, Stedman Graham, Bonnie McElveen-Hunter, Harvey Mackay, Oprah Winfrey, John Maxwell, Roger Staubach, and others who have overcome adversity to find their own success. Each of us shares a common goal: to help anyone establish the will and find their own path to success.

As we dive deeper into the concepts and structure that fashion the complicated quilt of the American dream, we should look carefully at the many obstacles that stand in the way. It sounds so simple: provide better education for all and encourage individuals to learn. So, what's stopping us, both society at large and the individual, from accessing the American dream? Why do so many believe that it is impossible? Are they afraid to try or are they afraid to fail? Let's explore one of the greatest obstacles for society *and* for the individual—the influence of fear.

CHAPTER 4

NOTHING TO FEAR: LIGHT THE DARKNESS WITH KNOWLEDGE

"Timendi causa est nescire."

"Ignorance is the cause of fear."

Seneca

We have all experienced fear at some point. Whether it is a fear of the unknown, a fear of failure, or simply being fearful of spiders or snakes, fear is an all-too-common emotion that stops us dead in our tracks. A powerful emotion, fear can threaten our ability to experience happiness or joy. The good news is that we can manage fear, a wholly internal emotion that simply resides in our minds. Each of us has a responsibility to ourselves and to our fellow citizens to disallow fear from becoming the reason we do not progress.

Fear comes in many forms, residing on both the macro and micro levels. We can fear as a person, as a family, or as a country. Our inability to manage fear on the personal level can be our greatest obstacle to fully experiencing the American dream. Sometimes, fear is contagious, quickly spreading from person to person, influencing one person after the other in monumental ways. This collective fear can even represent a grave threat to freedom and to our democracy.

During WWII, Winston Churchill recognized that fear was the tool of our enemies, both internal and external: "Your greatest fears are created by your imagination. Don't give in to them."

Franklin D. Roosevelt, during the worst of the Great Depression, brought hope to the American people in his inaugural address. He is famous for his quote that remains a powerful admonishment even today. The president, hoping to psychologically boost the American people in a time of tremendous despair, powerfully asserted, "The only thing we have to fear is fear itself." Freedom itself, whether one's personal freedom or the freedom of a nation, depends on our ability to overcome fear. Fear is a cancer that eats us from within. Roosevelt was addressing the negative cycle that gripped America at the time, but fear remains a continued challenge for individuals and for society at large.

We see the power of fear in our lives every day. The news is full of scary things. War, crime, disease, and the economy are all topics that can generate fear and concern. In the hands of those with a motive or agenda, fear can be weaponized. It is a powerful tool to motivate or manipulate. We are all vulnerable to this influence, but the most powerful antidote is knowledge. What makes a child fear the dark? The unknown. Turn on the light, and their fear disappears once they realize no monster is in the room. For all of us, at any age, knowledge is that shining light. With knowledge we can manage our fear or eliminate it completely.

Shining a light on any issue, uncovering the root cause, and determining the true nature of the risk is the best way to eliminate fear or at least to diagnose the validity or urgency of any given threat. A politician appealing to a broad electorate has a choice: they can build a platform on a foundation of hope or they can use fear to encourage their constituents to rally around their cause. Throughout history, we've seen that hope will generally prevail in a democratic electorate, but we must recognize that fear can also be an effective tool and sometimes will sway an electorate in surprising ways. Fear, whether based on fact or fiction, can cause inertia—the tendency to do nothing—and leave the status quo in place. Our objective, as individuals and as a society, must be to reverse this cycle of fear using knowledge to create hope.

Seeking knowledge is the same as turning on a light. When confronted by fear, if we seek knowledge to help us eliminate fear and strive for truth rather than fall back into anger and frustration; only then can we turn our fear into a medium for hope. Turning ignorance into a learning experience gives us a better chance of turning inertia into opportunity. This is the fundamental pathway to the American dream.

Unequivocally, fear threatens our ability to thrive, dream, and pursue all this life has to offer. So, if we are going to extinguish fear, or at least prevent it from influencing our lives, we must first understand it.

THE CRIPPLING FUNCTION OF "CAVEMAN" FEAR

Many types of fear exist. They appear in many shapes and sizes and through a variety of different influences. The better we are at recognizing them, the more adept we can be to shield ourselves from their impact. However, for purposes of our conversation, one type of fear seems to influence us the most. It is the most basic of all fears: the "caveman" fear, a practical fear born of self-preservation that generates a fight or flight response in all mammals. The human response may be more thoughtful than the response of our family pet, but fear will evoke the same instinctive reaction. We feel this fear in the spur of the moment, causing our instinctual brain to react in a way that is meant to help us survive the threat. It is the "encounter a bear in the woods" type of fear, where all you intend to do is make it out alive, even if it means running faster than your friend!

As humans, we should have enough knowledge to better assess risk, but the fundamental survival instincts lay just below the surface.

When the lion or tiger approaches us in the wild, our fear triggers the fight or flight instinct that could make the difference between surviving or becoming our aggressor's dinner. Our ancestors certainly needed this type of fear to protect them from natural predators. This instinctual fear was a product of the environment in which they lived, making them alert and responsive to the everyday threats that humans faced.

Today, we have few natural predators, yet the basic survival instinct remains. Our response to fear is too often relegated to the same fight or flight instincts that kept us from being eaten. Fight or flight, in today's world, is less necessary and could be self-destructive when dealing with the fear of an upcoming test or a boardroom presentation. The more prepared we are (that is, the more knowledge we have), the less likely we are to devolve into aggression or flight. When less prepared or doubtful of our own knowledge, the instinctive "fight" may be manifested in irrational behaviors, defensiveness, or anger. Alternatively, that fear could trigger an instinctive "flight," causing avoidance or denial of the challenge before us.

Let's explore the scientific and physiological reasons for such behavior. To avoid becoming lunch for a saber-toothed tiger, our ancestors needed a highly developed region of the brain called the amygdala, the "fear center." The central nucleus of this important node regulates the fear response and controls the release of certain hormones that trigger our physical response to fear. The basal and lateral nuclei assist with learning and associative processes, specifically receiving audio and visual cues that may result in conditioned fear responses. Basically, our brains remain wired the same as our Stone Age ancestors. We can take the man out of the cave, but, we haven't taken the caveman out of the man.

As a result, while most of us live in a modern age without the physical threat of lions, tigers, and bears, we remain vulnerable to fear. The daily stress of work, family, or our environment may still trigger our fight or flight response. The caveman needed a well-developed amygdala for self-preservation. Today's modern human, in contrast, relies more on the prefrontal cortex for self-preservation. But for the shrinking of the amygdala and increased activity of the prefrontal cortex, the caveman would have never evolved into the more rational human of today. Fear of the unknown would have gripped the caveman and kept him tethered to his cave. In contrast, we can have a more rational response to fear. On the way to the moon, the crew of Apollo 13 experienced a catastrophic explosion that vented much of their oxygen supply overboard. If the amygdala took control of the astronauts aboard Apollo 13, the crew might have perished, but instead their prefrontal cortex took over and the astronauts were able to modulate their fear impulse and return safely to Earth.

DEVELOPING YOUR AVIATOR BRAIN

Just like the astronauts aboard Apollo 13, a pilot is trained to respond to in-flight emergencies. Every commercial pilot must undergo annual or biannual training, often training in flight simulators, to practice responses to emergency situations like engine fire, windshear, or cabin decompression, all of which can cause the airplane to crash. Their response is critical to the safety of passengers and crew. They practice repeatedly so that their conditioned response becomes muscle memory, and they act almost instinctively. They are moderating the fear response and replacing it with muscle memory to take over in an emergency. They replace fear with knowledge, preparation, and a conditioned response that evokes confidence. That confidence enhances our ability to excel in challenging times. In today's world, humanity could certainly use a little less caveman brain and a lot more aviator brain to better assess and respond to fear. When certain experiences or potential opportunities come along, our ability to manage fear becomes an asset rather than a liability.

To move further away from caveman fear, we must reprogram our brains for a more modernized and logical approach to the threats we face. Think of this as development of our aviator brain. Freedom, and the ability to fulfill our destiny of self-determination, requires us to reprogram our minds as we would reprogram a computer. The good news: Science shows that we can change our own response patterns. An alcoholic can control the impulse to consume alcohol through counseling and peer support. A victim of abuse can stop the cycle of pain by delving into the root cause of these issues and practicing a different response.

Reprogramming our fear is much the same process. Fear can be useful, as it was to the caveman, to keep us safe. It may keep us from attempting to cross a busy four-lane highway or playing with fire. Allowing fear to protect us from real threat is a positive thing. We should not totally abandon fear. We need it to survive, but we should use it sparingly and develop our aviator brain to better control how we deal with perceived threats.

The problem so many of us face is responding in fear to imaginary threats. Our minds can spin that circumstance into a monster threat that will trigger our native fight or flight response. This could manifest itself in anger or violence, or the fear could cause one to freeze like a deer in the headlights. Even an imaginary threat can trigger a full-blown panic. Most times, our ignorance surrounding a given situation is the root cause of that fear. We are frightened because we don't understand an unfamiliar situation. This fear of the unknown is difficult to control, but we can manage our own physical and mental responses.

When dealing with the unknown, our minds will race from one worry to the next. This negative cycle will torment us and often will derail our personal development or career aspirations. One of the most common fears is the fear of failure. It's embarrassing to fail, and failing may reinforce your beliefs that you don't measure up.

Student A has thoroughly prepared for the exam through diligent study. Still, this student is uncomfortable because they tend to panic under stress and sometimes freeze over a question until time runs out. To defeat this negative response, they develop a habit of building their own practice exams. The repeated practice helps them get to the point that they ace every exam in practice. Even the process of building the practice test gives them more exposure to the potential questions and helps them study. When the day arrives for their actual test, they walk in with confidence and have silenced the negative thoughts and doubts that would have otherwise derailed their success.

Student B, in contrast, spends more time worrying than studying and the results are self-evident. On exam day, Student B panics. Fear causes the student to mentally spiral over every question. They may grow angry with the teacher or the test itself. Often this reaction devolves into a victim mentality where the student blames everyone else for their poor performance. Even worse is the chance that the student will turn the blame inward and believe they are simply not smart enough or good enough to succeed.

The simple lesson here is that preparation leads to familiarity, or the aviator brain phenomenon, which can shield each of us from the adverse consequences of fear. The unknown will always cause anxiety and could potentially trigger a negative response. But the antidote to that anxiety is knowledge and preparation. Becoming familiar with things or increasing one's knowledge of the circumstance can generate calm and expel worries. Once we understand the unknown, replacing ignorance with knowledge of that specific unknown, then we replace fear with familiarity, allowing confidence to prevail.

COLLECTIVE FEAR AND ITS IMPACT ON SOCIETY

While we can strive to moderate our own individual fears, we are subject to the societal impact of fear among those around us. This is a powerful phenomenon and can affect us even when we wouldn't otherwise feel fear. As individuals, we are sometimes vulnerable to that childhood fear of the dark because we don't know what lurks ahead. As previously noted, if we shine a light into that darkness (that is, acquire knowledge that what is ahead will not harm us), and we are no longer afraid. Why would we be afraid, if we turn on the light?

Now, let's see what happens when we add more individuals to the equation. Plunge one hundred people into darkness and naturally, that causes the fear to multiply. While there may be a sense of safety in numbers, that could be shattered if individuals seek to protect themselves at others' expense. The zebra, when confronted by a lion, may trample other zebras while fighting to find safety in the center of the herd. When confronted with a threat, something similar can instinctively happen to humans. If unable to escape the threat, their fight instinct may take over and they turn fear into anger or even violence in response to the threat.

The human instinct is the same. Even the ancient philosophers were known to recognize the danger of fear and its impact of ignorance on society. Ibn Rushd, an Arab Andalusian philosopher whose name was often Latinized as Averroes, wrote about this cycle of fear in the twelfth century. A well-known quote about the equation of fear is often attributed to Averroes. "Ignorance leads to fear, fear leads to hate, and hate leads to violence. This is the equation." If the words of an ancient philosopher don't resonate, then perhaps the advice of Yoda in *Star Wars* will ring true. "Fear is the path to the dark side. Fear leads to anger. Anger leads to hate. Hate leads to suffering." The cycle looks something like this:

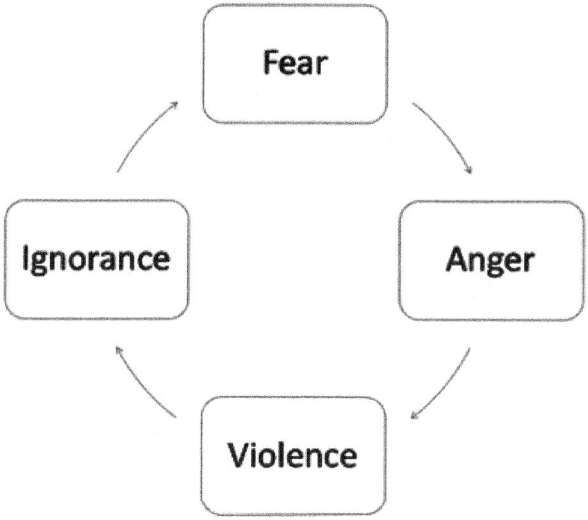

In his book *The Joy of Militant Ignorance,* Peter Michaelson describes human beings as "highly resistant to acquiring self-knowledge." "Our ego," he writes, "the turtle shell of our mind readily embraces willful, even militant, ignorance as self-protection." *Militant ignorance* is the fierce determination to remain ignorant and stuck in psychological darkness. (What comes to mind is the stereotype of the grumpy old man.)

Militant ignorance worsens when others reinforce it. That is precisely why a mob turns into a mob, transforming normally peaceful individuals into an angry, violent group. The group can take on its own sense of right and wrong, building confidence in individuals because they mirror the behavior of those around them. Militant ignorance is "one of the better definitions" of evil, according to M. Scott Peck, author of *The Road Less Traveled*. Often, a refusal to gain new knowledge can trigger the harm that we may do to ourselves or to others. Many of the challenges society faces can be traced to our individual and collective refusal to learn.

Let's take the environment as an example. We can all agree that pollution is bad. If we do irreparable damage to our planet, then we are clearly harming ourselves and future generations. This is seemingly self-evident. Yet why do so many hunters, fishermen, and lovers of the outdoors so strongly fight back against those they might call "tree-hugging" environmentalists? Why do concepts like "global warming" or "climate change" trigger fear, anger, and even violence on both sides of the argument? How is it possible that rational, informed people cannot come together on this important topic to find practical, rational solutions?

The human ego is very protective. When external forces challenge or threaten it, our ego becomes a champion of militant ignorance. While we may sometimes experience feelings of inadequacy, our egos are sometimes bolstered by the opinions or beliefs of those around us. As a result, we become steeped in a position or a belief that we are right because those around us may believe the same.

Imagine these two groups rallying around their cause. Those who are sometimes called "tree huggers" will unite around a belief that the planet is being destroyed and that we must cease this destructive behavior at all costs. In turn, those who might be called "climate deniers" may believe it is all a hoax propagated by those who want to take away our freedom. The ultimate irony is that any one individual, pulled from the fray, could agree that both "freedom" and "protection of the planet" are good things. They could agree separately that we should all work together toward rational decisions. Put that individual back in the group and the respective groupthink or tribal instinct may prevail.

The human ego protects the illusion of right and wrong, truth and falsehood. It will sometimes default to militant ignorance, blocking our willingness to accept new information and triggering an emotional fight instinct that causes us to defend rather than to learn. Members of a tribe will preserve the leader's ego in return for secondhand affirmation of their own. When operating through ego, we care less about facts and instead we care more about what preserves the illusion of knowing what is true and real. The ego protects us from our own dark side, our fear of inadequacy or our fear of being a know-nothing. In a tribal existence, everyday people feel the power to deny reality. When others join in the collective defiance, they boldly mock the truth, ignore science, eschew the facts, and threaten nonbelievers.

A personal commitment to learning is the antidote to militant ignorance and a solution to tribalism. Self-knowledge will develop our better selves, leading us away from incivility and hatred. Bestselling author Yuval Noah Harari addresses psychological ignorance in his book *21 Lessons for the 21st Century*. The book attempts to illuminate the core issues facing the world, addressing ignorance and its harmful effects.

Harari notes that "the world is becoming ever more complex, and people fail to realize just how ignorant they are of what's going on." Human rationality, he points out, is replaced by emotional reactions and intellectual shortcuts. "The best we can do under such conditions," he writes, "is to acknowledge our own individual ignorance." He points to groupthink and group loyalty as an explanation for widespread ignorance.

If our democracy doesn't survive, our own ignorance will likely take us down. Throughout history, ignorance has produced the evil we do to ourselves, to others, and to our world. Individually or collectively, ignorance and the fear that it produces has been one of the greatest failings of mankind. As a civilization we are at a critical juncture on the course of human evolution. The quality of life and the future of humanity will be determined by our ability to foster self-knowledge, and ultimately wisdom. This premise is at the heart of our belief that education is freedom.

In a famous interview in 1987, Margaret Thatcher said, "There is no such thing as society. There is [a] living tapestry of men and women...and the quality of our lives will depend upon how much each of us is prepared to take responsibility for ourselves." Therefore, our collective desire for the greater good becomes the bright light that will take away our fear.

If we replace ignorance with knowledge...
Then we can replace anger with understanding...
We can replace violence with peace...
We can replace fear with hope...

Do these things, and the cycle will look more like this:

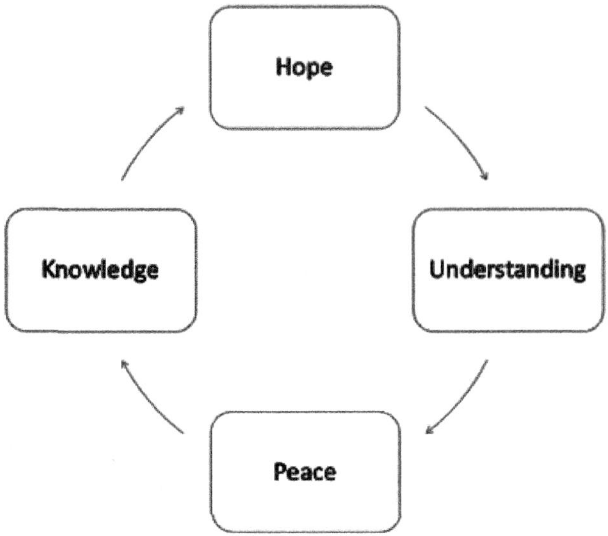

Thatcher shared a common belief that "society" cannot fix what we cannot fix within ourselves. We are society, the cumulative behavior of each of us individually. For society to improve, each of us must individually improve. For society to flourish, each of us individually must flourish.

Self-determination of a people, whether the American people or the people of the world, must begin with "self." We each have a choice: We can accept the obstacles, negative influences, and adversity around us and wallow in despair and hopelessness. Or we can take responsibility for our own destiny by doing our best to live our fullest lives and make our greatest contributions to the world around us.

Your fear may trigger a negative response to this very notion. It may trigger that voice in your head that says the system is rigged against you and that nothing you can do will help. It may cause you to ridicule those who even suggest that your fate is in your own hands. Your reaction may be that "we" are right and "they" are wrong. For now, I hope you will silence that persistent voice and suspend your disbelief because the pathway to freedom is in *your* hands. Ultimately, I hope you'll agree, the pathway to freedom is in our hands.

In the words of Aristotle, "He who has overcome his fears will truly be free." That is not to say it will be easy or even come naturally. Fear is real, and it can impact us to various degrees. In fact, many of us have lived in a cycle of fear for most of our lives, allowing our caveman brain to control otherwise logical and well-thought-out decisions. However, as we begin to better understand ourselves and the forces that influence our decisions, we can replace fear with a shining light of opportunity.

SECTION II
WHAT TO LEARN

Below I will offer a formula to obliterate fear in its many unique shapes and sizes. Overcoming fear is a prerequisite to a successful life. Whether you are a student on your educational journey, a parent who wants the best future for their children, an entrepreneur trying to chart a path to success, or simply someone who wants greater fulfillment in life, these first three critical success factors may help you chart the journey. They are very simply *what* you must learn to be *able* to *learn*. They include:

- **Change:** I have a favorite expression, appropriate for anyone who wants to be CEO of their own life. *Change Equals Opportunity*. Most people have an adverse reaction to change. Acceptance of change and the ability to respond in a positive, proactive fashion is the biggest challenge; but also the single biggest opportunity for an individual or an organization. Adversity does not define the individual, but one's response to adversity does. That response can separate winners from losers.
- **Confidence:** We all suffer from insecurity, making us weak and often unable to achieve our highest potential. Fear and insecurity lead to ignorance and failure. Knowledge is the best antidote because armed with information, confidence can prevail within anyone. To overcome the pervasive fear of failure that holds many of us back, I have adopted a favorite quote from Nelson Mandela: "I never lose. I either win or learn."
- **Clarity:** The ability to turn complex problems into understandable parts that can lead to simple solutions is the art of "clarity." Achieving simplicity is a difficult task for most people, but it is essential to moving forward. The fundamental prerequisite for clarity is effective communication, both inbound communication (listening) and outbound communication (speaking).

> Clarity in both giving and receiving information is an essential element of learning and a prerequisite to our ultimate success.

If I was to attribute any of the success that I've enjoyed in life—personally, professionally, or even academically—it would be the recognition that *change equals opportunity*; the *confidence* to deal with even the most challenging circumstance; and the *clarity* of thought to illuminate the path forward. I recognize these simple strengths as a gift that I can pay forward and share with the world. I believe that anyone, even in the most adverse circumstances, can overcome the odds and find their own freedom with these simple gifts.

In the next few chapters, we will explore each of these critical success factors in more detail. They define *what* we need to learn before progressing on our journey of lifelong learning. Each of the following chapters will increase your awareness, and that's where the learning begins.

CHAPTER 5

CHANGE: CHANGE EQUALS OPPORTUNITY

"Ad Astra Per Aspera"

Latin for "To the stars through difficulties"

John James Ingalls

We have all experienced the pain of change. In stark contrast, we have also likely experienced the joy that can accompany a positive change. It is easy to see how change, a constant in life, is a double-sided coin that can sometimes land your way and other times not. Regardless of how the coin falls, understanding change and responding to it in a healthy way can be a tremendous resource. A best-kept secret is that adaptation to change is often the jet fuel that propels the American dream.

I speak from experience because I *live* the American dream. Frankly, I can only imagine where I would be in life had it not been for the great opportunity that change ushered into my existence. How does a child born into impossible circumstances rise from the rubble of a broken family, a shack without running water, and abject poverty? The answer is "turning change into opportunity." A change of circumstances. A change of perspective. A change in mindset.

This was my path to experience the American dream and it can be yours. I learned to embrace change and to recognize that change does equal opportunity. Nothing in life is stagnant, and like the river that is constantly moving, so is change. Early on, I decided to become the CEO of my own life by recognizing that no one else was responsible for my future. It was my destiny to seize. No one, and I mean no one, was going to write my story but me. As a child, I knew I wasn't an "Albert Einstein," but as the genius physicist was known to say, "The measure of intelligence is the ability to change."

It took many years to learn that valuable lesson. The lesson is not only that change equals opportunity, but that overcoming adversity builds strength. The stronger you are, the more adept you will be at navigating obstacles and misfortunes. The Bible even references adversity in James 1:12, stating, "Blessed is the one who perseveres under trial because, having stood the test, that person will receive the crown of life that the Lord has promised to those who love Him" (NIV). While adversity can translate into strength, it can be hard to see the upside while under duress. Many different forms of change exist. The toughest of all is the gut-wrenching, life-altering, soul-crushing change that makes you wonder, *What did I do to deserve this?* It was only in the face of adversity that I came to realize, it is not the change that matters, it is our response to change that counts. Our adaptation to change is the key to survival in school, in business, and in life.

BECOMING A CEO: CHANGE EQUALS OPPORTUNITY

Growing up, I simply accepted that change was a part of life. It seemed that around every corner was some event that would disrupt my life. As if poverty alone was not adversity enough, I had to deal with that host of issues that no child should have to endure. Little did I know that such adversity would prepare me to deal with change throughout my career and give me the strength needed to face any obstacles before me.

Not long after beginning a career with Gulf Oil Corporation, the company merged with Chevron, and I found myself unsure of the future. At Gulf, my career was on a rocket-like trajectory. My first role was in corporate planning, working with an elite group of professionals exploring mergers and acquisition opportunities. I was then asked to participate on a Chevron/Gulf team defining the strategy of the newly merged refining and marketing operations. I was part of the merger team defining the strategy of the newly merged refining and marketing operations of Chevron. During this time, a senior executive from Chevron put an arm around my shoulder. He said, "Young man, I'm not sure how you got this role but you're going to have to step back now and pay some dues here at Chevron. Just keep your head down, stay out of trouble, and you too could become a 'senior manager' one day." Frustrated by this development, I wondered about my fate. I was offered an opportunity to join The Southland Corporation to help them turn-around their newly acquired company, CITGO Petroleum.

Southland was the parent company of 7-Eleven and acquired CITGO to secure gasoline supply for its 7-Eleven stores. Joining the company via CITGO Petroleum sounded like a wonderful career path. That is, until a year later the company sold CITGO to PDVSA (Petróleos de Venezuela), the government run oil company of Venezuela. Again, I faced "change." But as fate would have it, the CEO of The Southland Corporation reached out to offer me a new role within the parent company, managing all the retail gasoline operations for 7-Eleven stores. When one door closes, another will open if we give it the chance. Once again, change worked out to my benefit. If I had my head down or saw those inevitable changes as a setback, one never knows where my career may have drifted. Instead, I stayed positive and worked harder despite the uncertainty.

Opportunity, and change, presented itself once again when 7-Eleven's parent company took a big step by going private. The Southland Corporation, a NYSE company, decided that it would execute a leveraged buyout and took on $4 billion of debt to become a private company. Their timing wasn't great, executing this plan during the financial crisis of 1987. The interest rate on that $4 billion loan (junk bonds actually) was over 16 percent. This would be like taking a mortgage on your home but being unable to pay the interest cost of that mortgage. It was only a matter of time before the parent company of 7-Eleven was forced to file for bankruptcy protection. As a relatively young man, I wondered once again what would become of my career.

I sat down with John P. Thompson, chairman of the company, to ask for his advice. His advice was sound. He acknowledged that people had a hard time dealing with "change" and that companies were no different. He explained that The Southland Corporation, parent of 7-Eleven, was a company founded by his father, Joe C. Thompson. He then shared the story of the humble beginnings of 7-Eleven. Starting as The Southland Ice Company, they sold large blocks of ice to neighbors for their "ice box." Then, in 1927, someone invented the "Frigidaire refrigerator" eviscerating their market. If the company didn't adapt to change, it would have gone out of business in just a few years. Instead, he said, they embraced that change and asked their customers what else they needed to buy "conveniently," adding bread and milk to their product assortment. They realized that they weren't in the business of selling ice. They were in the business of selling "convenience." Ice was just one item that people needed conveniently at that time, but convenience needs change every day.

He reminded me that 7-Eleven's core business was "convenience," but the company was no longer keeping up with convenience trends for the 1990s and had stopped changing with the times. Over time the company had settled into selling convenience items like beer, soft drinks and cigarettes. Many other retail stores were now selling the same items and 7-Eleven sales were declining. He reminded me that 7-Eleven wasn't in the beer and cigarette business; it was in the "convenience" business. The need for convenience, he said, would never die. Thompson explained that my job was to embrace that change and to find products that would satisfy our customers' need for convenience. If able to do so, then the company, and certainly my own career, would flourish.

He was right! I decided to stay with the company and became obsessed with "change," searching all over the world for those items that would help the company satisfy its core mission of convenience. Rather than putting my head down and feeling sorry for myself or my company because of the bankruptcy, I worked harder and smarter to find a way to succeed.

As we emerged from bankruptcy in 1991, I was fortunate to be given the opportunity to lead the company's strategic planning process. I was able to craft a new strategy for the company going forward, making "adaptation to change" a part of the company's mission. Shortly thereafter, I was given the opportunity to become Chief Financial Officer of the new entity, 7-Eleven, Inc. Here was another change that I had to embrace. As a political science major in college and a with a marketing concentration in business school, I was ill equipped for the role of a public company CFO. I remember going home that evening and searching for my textbook from the one accounting class I took in graduate school! Thankfully, I had a strong controller and an excellent audit partner at Price Waterhouse who were able to help me learn on the job. In the next chapter, we will talk about confidence. This was a time in my career when confidence became a strong asset.

After a few years, I was promoted to chief operating officer and then, in 1999, they announced my succession to CEO. I became CEO of 7-Eleven, Inc., embracing change and recognizing that CEO isn't only an acronym for chief executive officer, but could also mean that *Change Equals Opportunity*. Each of those career changes was enabled because of change, some of it good and some of it bad. In the end, by embracing those changes I had the privilege of learning the 7-Eleven business from both the operating and financial sides. I then had the chance to craft a long-term plan for the business coming out of bankruptcy. Later, as CFO, I had the opportunity to finance that plan while improving the company's balance sheet. Next, as COO (Chief Operating Officer) I had the opportunity to execute the plan and put the strategy in place. Finally, as chief executive, I had the privilege of leading the company's growth domestically and internationally. The entire journey was a learning experience and a case study in adaptation to change.

Looking back, I realize that the change I had to deal with in youth prepared me for later in life, when change would become the driver of personal and professional opportunity. Rather than being afraid of change or focusing on the "why me?" aspect of change, I was able to embrace it and see it for what it is—an opportunity to move forward. While seldom clear at the time, it is with hindsight that we can sometimes understand that change worked out to our benefit and that there was nothing to fear. Much of this comes down to our attitude, since it is our response to change rather than the change itself that often matters most. Let me show you what I mean.

CHANGE BEGINS WITH YOUR ATTITUDE

How do we learn to navigate and manage what can only be described as unexpected, unintended, or painful change? Think of your favorite sports team, down by several runs and heading into the last innings or final quarter of the game. Are they looking at this deficit with negativity and despair? Or do they put on their rally caps, take the game plan to the chalkboard for a winning play, and come out fighting to turn adversity into opportunity for the win? We all know the difference is that champions look to find a way to win. They strive to come out on top, despite any odds that may not seem to be in their favor.

Oprah Winfrey, another member of the Horatio Alger Association said, "The greatest discovery of all time is that a person can change his future by merely changing his attitude." Attitude comes from within. It is not how the world perceives you, but rather, how you perceive the world. Do we face change with fear or with optimism? Do we feel mistreated, abused, and unable to succeed? Often our victim mentality is grounded in fear—fear of change, fear of failure, fear of our inability to control our own destinies. Fear is normal, and you are simply human if you feel fear in relation to change. It is not the change itself, but rather how you choose to react or respond to change is what defines you—in other words, your attitude.

We all know someone who seems to have a positive outlook no matter what the world dishes out. We also know those who seem defeated by their own problems. Which of these two people would you rather spend time with? If you didn't know either of these two people, which one would you guess might reach their goals? These are basic questions, of course, but they often provide us with guidance about why our attitudes can be such game-changers in life. To many, across all religions or none, this can be a matter of "faith."

This simple concept from a novel (*The Alchemist*) is a thread that runs through every religion. In the book, Paulo Coelho captures the spirit of faith in a non-denominational way, stating, "When you want something, all the universe conspires in helping you achieve it." Faith is the cornerstone for many religions, including Christianity, Judaism, Islam, or Buddhism. Each of us may place our faith in God, Buddha, or the Universe, but it all starts from within. Prayer doesn't work if it doesn't come from inside. Meditation doesn't work if it doesn't turn inward. The universe will not "conspire to make it happen" if you don't know what you want. For a prayer to be fulfilled, a change may be required; but if you're unwilling to change, then the fulfillment of prayer may not come to pass. Interesting, isn't it? Manifestation without action often leads to nothing other than maintaining the status quo. That's something to think about as you sit idly and pray your conditions will change without action. That may sound harsh, but it was largely the combination of mindset and action that helped me navigate my own life journey and can also help yours. My faith, not just a belief in God but also belief in myself, was essential to that journey.

In exchange for a life of grace, a monk must give up all worldly possessions. Most of us would draw the line at this requirement for fear of losing what we have. Giving up all of one's worldly possessions is the most profound expression of faith, but it is also the most profound rejection of fear. There is no guarantee that the monk will be granted redemption, grace, or eternal life. But the monk must set this fear aside and embrace the change necessary to free his mind and soul of worldly matters. They do this with confidence. Why? Because they are believers. Their attitude is one of humility, with their goal being an inscription into the book of eternal life. The monk knows that the secret to embracing change is to overcome the fear of losing something. We may fear losing the little we already have. It is natural to resist the change that happens to us and, likewise, to resist the change we must make to ourselves.

"The only people who like change are wet babies," said author Harvey Mackay. Mackay knows a few things about adversity and wrote the bestselling book, *Swim with the Sharks Without Being Eaten Alive*. "Many times, in order to survive we have to start a change process," he wrote. "Change, for most people, is an unnerving experience. But as the old saying goes, change is inevitable. It is one of the only constants in life. I have said before, it is easy to change things. It is not so easy to change people. Most organizations won't survive if they don't learn how to change as they grow and adapt to market conditions."

CHANGE IS NOT AN EXCUSE, IT IS A WAY OF LIFE

We sometimes use change as an excuse. It gives us permission to quit or to blame others for our misfortunes. If we can see adversity, whatever it may be, as a spark to give us strength or to fuel a change in ourselves, then we *can* turn that adversity into opportunity. The act of embracing change defies the odds, not because it is insurmountable but because others will tell us the journey is impossible. You've heard it here first—despite your desire to make meaningful and lasting change, other people will attempt to persuade you to believe that change is an impossibility. Often, the voices of doubt ring in our heads. The word "can't" becomes etched in our brains. We must turn, however, to a belief that anything is possible—because it is. While others can fabricate fear for you, the less you listen to these internal or external voices, the better off you will be.

Speaking of approaching adversity with a take-charge attitude, consider the challenges faced by Nelson Mandela in South Africa. Imprisoned for his beliefs and his fight against apartheid, Mandela could have withered away in despair behind bars. Instead, he turned adversity into opportunity and studied law while in prison. At one point, a new prison warden discovered Mandela and his fellow inmates surrounded by law books and engaged in a case study of international law. He chastised Mandela and his peers for turning the prison into a school, which is exactly what Mandela had accomplished. From unthinkable adversity, Mandela created opportunity for himself and others, emerging from prison more knowledgeable and competent to serve as South Africa's president—a role neither he nor his peers could have dreamed possible from the dank surroundings of their prison cells.

Mandela turned change into opportunity and adversity into strength. He is a shining example of recognizing the need for change and then making it a way of life. Of course, he could have withered away in jail and given up any real hope for his release. Instead, he chose opportunity over adversity. He took control of his circumstances, as bleak as they seemed, and owned them. He could have easily made every excuse in the book, but there was no "give up" in him.

Much like Mandela serving time in jail, if the student growing up on the South Side of Chicago feels that the system is stacked against him, that feeling may be justified. The system, it has been said, is rigged against some and (depending on your view) broken. Despite your circumstances, you are the owner and narrator of your fate. Should this be an excuse to give up? Should that student give in to the lure of a gang showing them the "easy" path to freedom through crime or anarchy? Should "going against the odds" be an excuse or an opportunity? I will let you decide.

THE PAIN OF CHANGE

The path to dealing with change is seldom easy. At times, it is gut-wrenching. Consider the case of fifteen-year-old schoolgirl Malala Yousafzai who was shot in the head by Taliban gunmen in 2012. A catastrophic incident to say the least, she was attacked because she spoke up for the rights of girls to receive education. This was literally a shot heard around the world, and the general population reacted in horror to this senseless act of violence. After weeks of intensive care and after undergoing a delicate brain surgery, Malala survived. She celebrated her sixteenth birthday by addressing the United Nations. Like Madonna or Cher, she is now known worldwide by her first name only. Former British Prime Minister Gordon Brown called her "an icon of courage and hope."

Growing up in Pakistan, Malala's world was not one of wealth or privilege. It was, however, a life dominated by learning, with a family who encouraged and supported her thirst for knowledge. "She [Malala] was precocious, confident, assertive," said Adnan Aurangzeb, a member of the Pakistani Parliament. "A young person with the drive to achieve something in life." Her drive came from an awareness that securing one of a few professional roles in Pakistan would allow women to work outside of the home. "For my brothers it was easy to think about the future. They can be anything they want," Malala said. "But for me it was hard and for that reason I wanted to become educated and empower myself with knowledge."

Ziauddin Yousafzai, Malala's father, must have known that his daughter's high profile in the valley put her at some risk, even though he could not have foreseen the outcome. "Malala's voice was the most powerful voice in Swat because the biggest victim of the Taliban was girls' schools and girls' education and few people talked about it," he said. "When she used to speak about education, everybody gave it importance."

"One child, one teacher, one book, one pen can change the world," Malala said. "When I looked at 400 youth and people from more than 100 countries...I said that I am not only talking to the people of America and the other countries, but I am also talking to every person in the world."

Malala has overcome the worst of humanity and the worst of adversity. She could have disappeared in anonymity and accepted the role of victim. Instead, she rose and saw education as her continued path to freedom. Her journey allowed her to also experience the best of humanity, from the doctors who cared for her to the students around the world who were inspired by her message. Malala believes that education is freedom...all over the world. It is time for each of us to embrace change and take personal responsibility for our learning. It is time to turn change into opportunity.

RESPONDING TO CHANGE: THE ANSWER IS WITHIN

Fear is real. So is adversity. The pain that you may experience with both is real as well. However, none of these things define us. They are external factors that may affect us and will certainly shape us. The key to embracing change and becoming the CEO of your own life begins from within. Whatever your faith, whatever your belief, whatever your background, you must begin with a belief in yourself.

President Barack Obama said, "Change will not come if we wait for some other person or if we wait for some other time. We are the ones we are waiting for. We are the change we seek." So, with that said, why is change the focus of the first chapter in this road map? Because if you cannot navigate change, there isn't much else to discuss.

If you're Nelson Mandela and put in jail for your beliefs, you don't waste away in prison. Rather, you study the law and emerge as a better person for the adversity you just faced. If you're Steve Jobs and get thrown out of the very company you built, you work even harder to come up with better ideas and return to make your old company an even greater success. It is often the path of most resistance, but that path could be your number one shot at accomplishing what may have seemed impossible.

If this was easy, anyone could do it. Hard makes us stronger. It builds the muscles we need to traverse this crazy thing called life. Hard makes us better if we let it. We can emerge a better person. They say that a broken bone grows back even stronger than it was before it suffered the break, and the same is true with our minds as we relate to overcoming adversity. We grow back stronger and better if we learn from the experience, if we have the heart to endure it.

Believe in yourself, and others will believe in you. Believe in your ability to turn change into opportunity, and you will find a better path. If you want something, the universe will indeed conspire to make it happen...but you must be proactive in making it happen. To change, to embrace change, and to turn change into opportunity comes down to one's confidence.

Be confident to win. Be confident to overcome. Be confident to succeed.

CHAPTER 6

CONFIDENCE: KNOW YOU CAN

"The moment you doubt whether you can fly,
you cease for ever to be able to do it."

J. M. Barrie

We all know that one person, the one who walks into a room and radiates a transcendental type of energy. You can feel it, and it pierces through everyone they touch and draws those people to them. It's like a powerful magnet, and you constantly want more. As you look to describe the experience, only one word comes to mind: confidence.

I am one of those people who believes that anything is possible. But that strong sense of confidence didn't come naturally. Like everyone, I have my share of insecurities. I've never believed that I was smarter than the average bear, nor stronger or more capable. Instead, I believed that I could accomplish anything by simply out-trying or out-working anyone in the field. I wasn't the best athlete but during baseball or football practice I would simply work harder than the rest. When running sprints or laps around the track, I would always try to be first. When asked to clean the parking lot at my first job at McDonald's, I would run around the lot to pick up the trash. On the baseball field, I was rewarded with a starting position.

At McDonald's, I was rewarded with a shift manager role. Neither of these opportunities came from being better or smarter than my peers, but instead because I simply worked harder than the rest.

My own sense of confidence likely ties back to the adversity that dominated my early years. Did personal setbacks create that confidence, or did confidence help me deal with the setbacks? The answer is both. Dealing with change and the confidence to move forward go hand in hand. They are complimentary but not necessarily innate. Confidence, like muscle memory, is built through experience. Within both adversity and failure are learnings. From adversity, we learn that the world will not end because of some terrible thing that may happen. Dealing with adversity can build strength, resilience, and, yes, confidence. Failure is learning *if* we can learn from our mistakes. The cumulative effect of both adversity and failure contributed to the strength of confidence that serves me well today.

It was that confidence that led me to the opportunity to transform Blockbuster, Inc. I had just completed a successful twenty-one-year career with 7-Eleven and led the sale of the company to Ito-Yokado, its Japanese licensee. With a tenfold increase in shareholder value during my term as chief executive at 7-Eleven, I was ready for a new challenge. Armed with experience in the use of technology for business transformation and significant experience in business turnarounds, I decided to take the role of Chairman and CEO of Blockbuster in July of 2007.

The iconic brand that was part of everyone's life during the '80s and '90s was struggling in the new millennium. Netflix had created a new model for ordering DVDs by mail and Blockbuster responded with its own by-mail offering. Meanwhile, the stores were getting a bit tired, in-stock availability of new releases was erratic causing sales to decline, and the company's earnings were struggling under a debt load of $1 billion. During my first week on the job, I realized that the situation would be more challenging than expected. The company had just violated a bank covenant (like missing several mortgage payments and having the bank threaten to take your home). Still, I had confidence in the turnaround plan going forward and a longer-term plan to transform the company from physical stores to a digital streaming service. The business was fundamentally like 7-Eleven. Blockbuster was not in the business of DVD rentals, but instead it was in the business of "convenient access to media entertainment." I remembered the words of John Thompson, my mentor at 7-Eleven. "Products will come and go but the need for convenience will never die," he said. The mission? Provide access to Blockbuster customers with media entertainment where they want, when they want, and how they want it.

The first year at Blockbuster went exceptionally well. We acquired a streaming video company called Movielink, one of the first digital streaming companies that was a collaboration between five major movie studios who hoped to control content in the future video streaming market. This was a huge win because, with this transaction, the studios were identifying Blockbuster as their preferred partner as they looked to the future of streaming video. *Wired* magazine said of the acquisition, "Blockbuster announced its acquisition of the studio backed video-on-demand site Movielink. It's not just the small studios who've helped Blockbuster land this blow either—with the site boasting licensed content from Sony Pictures, Universal, Warner Bros., MGM, and Paramount, this could easily put the battle weary rental company in the lead. Make no bones about it—Blockbuster CEO Jim Keyes is more than prepared to tap this union's potential too."[11]

Meanwhile, we focused on improving the stores' business to provide the cash flow needed to build our future digital offering. After the first year, we had nearly doubled earnings. Confidence was carrying the day as we looked forward to a successful turnaround and were very well positioned to compete into the future.

11 Terrence Russell, "Blockbuster Gains Ground with Movielink Acquisition," *Wired*, August 9, 2007, https://www.wired.com/2007/08/although-its-no/.

Our Blockbuster offering at the time was called *Total Access*. We had movies in stores, by-mail (like Netflix), via kiosk (like Redbox), and via streaming through Blockbuster On Demand.

That's when *change* reared its ugly head. We were celebrating a successful third quarter earnings release in the fall of 2008 when Lehman Brothers announced their collapse, and the banking market and economy virtually shut down. Blockbuster had $1 billion of debt with one third of it due (i.e., needing to be refinanced) by the first quarter of 2009. Our investment banking advisors warned that it may be impossible to refinance the debt. The Wall Street rating agencies, Moody's and Standard and Poor's, gave us good news by upgrading our corporate debt ratings. "This two notch upgrade reflects the company's improved recovery prospects as a result of the company's notable operating improvements," was the press release from Moody's Investor Service. During the same announcement of that good news, however, Moody's declared the company a potential bankruptcy risk. Their caution to investors, they said, "considers that despite a notable improvement in operating income and a reduction in leverage, Blockbuster still remains highly leveraged and is faced with the burden of refinancing in a challenging credit environment."[12]

This is when my own confidence was tested. The sharks came out to circle the company. The press became aggressive. We had significant positive cash flow and no immediate risk to our liquidity, but the rumors of our demise were swirling. Despite my reassurance to investors, the *New York Post* printed a half-page photo of my image with a Pinocchio nose and the headline "Blockbusted," because they "were told by sources" that the company was going to file for bankruptcy. In a matter of weeks, I had gone from the company's white knight to being blamed for the company's problems.

Amid this crisis, I attended an event hosted by Microsoft at the home of their Chairman, Bill Gates. I was a bit starstruck at the

12 Moody's Global Credit Research, August 14, 2008. Approximately $1.2 billion of rated debt affected.

gathering of corporate luminaries like Gates, Jeff Bezos of Amazon, Meg Whitman of eBay, and others. While in line for food, Warren Buffett was also getting a plate of his own. I modestly approached him to shake his hand. To my surprise, he remembered me from 7-Eleven and had not long before congratulated me for the Horatio Alger award by sending me a copy of his own autobiography. When he asked how I was doing post-7-Eleven, I became almost apologetic about my fate. I explained that Blockbuster was struggling from the financial crisis and that my plans for a digital offering had to be delayed until we corrected the financial situation. I told him about the *New York Post* article and that I now questioned my decision to take on this challenge. Warren looked at me with that "look" that he has, and the Oracle of Omaha asked me if I would rather be on the bench watching from the sidelines or in the arena with mud on my face.

He was right. I was glad to be in the arena. It reminded me of the famous Theodore Roosevelt speech about the man in the arena:

> *It is not the critic who counts; not the man who points out how the strong man stumbles, or where the doer of deeds could have done them better. The credit belongs to the man who is actually in the arena, whose face is marred by dust and sweat and blood; who strives valiantly; who errs; who comes short again and again, because there is no effort without error and shortcoming; but who does actually strive to do the deeds; who knows great enthusiasms, the great devotions; who spends himself in a worthy cause; who at the best knows in the end the triumph of high achievement, and who at the worse, if he fails, at least fails while daring greatly, so that his place shall never be with those cold and timid souls who neither know victory nor defeat.*

Thanks to Warren's advice, I stayed in the arena. I fought the good fight against incredible odds and protected the company from those who would have subjected it to liquidation.

It was clear that we needed help to facilitate a digital transition. One opportunity was a potential deal with Philippe Dauman, Chairman and CEO of Viacom, who was orchestrating a plan to partner with Blockbuster for exclusive rights to digital/streaming content. This deal would have given Blockbuster exclusive rights to 60 percent of all catalogue (i.e., older movies) and potentially would have left Netflix with little digital content to stream. The deal would have been ideal but for the price tag. Blockbuster would have had to commit to $100 million per year to secure the exclusive rights to this content.

When we presented the opportunity to the Blockbuster board of directors, they pushed back. At the time, there was no clear market for streaming content because the internet remained very weak, and the timetable for development of relevant technologies (both in Wi-Fi connectivity and hardware devices) and consumer adoption remained uncertain. The Blockbuster board of directors voted down this collaboration, allowing Netflix to then acquire digital rights on a non-exclusive basis. Declining the opportunity also provided Netflix with a window to succeed. We missed that opportunity but had others in the wings.

The most exciting opportunity for Blockbuster came through discussions with Google. At the time, Google was in conflict with the movie studios over movie and television content being streamed free via YouTube. Our collaboration opportunity was to partner with Google so that all "free" content would be available via YouTube, and any "paid" content would be available via Blockbuster. Blockbuster On Demand would sit side by side with YouTube, and every Google search for content would be directed to one of those two channels. This collaboration would have facilitated the acquisition of exclusive content described above.

The Blockbuster board approved and signed the definitive agreement, which was in the hands of the Google board when the *LA Times* published an article speculating on the potential bankruptcy of Blockbuster. While it wasn't an accurate portrayal of Blockbuster's financial situation, the perception of financial difficulties was enough to cause the Google board to decline the transaction. I remember the call from Nikesh Arora, a senior executive at Google, explaining that they would have to pass on the deal until Blockbuster could achieve financial stability. Sadly, it was another missed opportunity for collaboration that could have changed the face of media content availability all over the world.

The added pressure of the debt refinancing during the 2009 financial market collapse ultimately forced a restructuring. We accomplished a difficult though successful restructuring and sale of the company to Dish Network. In doing so, we hoped they could better accomplish the digital transformation. I wish I could point to this as a success, but unfortunately the outcome wasn't the one that I had envisioned. The timing was still a bit early for digital streaming and Dish was unable to execute its strategy. Their ambitious plan was to bypass the internet and move straight to mobility for more convenient and effective media access. Their plan required robust telecom capabilities (at least 5G) which are barely in place in America today. They eventually closed the stores, and the Blockbuster brand remains in mothballs today but for a single licensed store in Bend, Oregon, that keeps the lights on and the legacy alive!

The lesson here is that confidence can open doors. It can help you stay the course in troubled waters and can give you the strength to lead. It can also be difficult to maintain your confidence during the storm. During the most difficult times, your confidence will be challenged from all fronts. Seeing your name disparaged in the press or being wrongly accused by those on the sidelines can be an assault on your self-esteem, making it difficult to remain confident. The lesson here is important. I was able to stay the course and to maintain both confidence and self-esteem *because* I came to realize that the attacks and the criticism were not personal.

Challenges to your confidence will come from all directions for any number of reasons. In this case, it was just "business." Sometimes it will be the projection of others prompted by their own insecurity. Sometimes it will be jealousy. Sometimes it will be an ulterior motive, driven by conflicting objectives or even by those with a financial motivation to see you fail. This is where your personal identity will come into play. Management guru Peter Drucker was famous for his reflection on leadership. "Management," he says, "is doing things right; leadership is doing the right things." If you do your homework, assemble the best information available and proceed with confidence even then you may fall short of your target. In this situation, your self-esteem becomes important to preserve. Learn from your mistakes and move on knowing that you'll live to fight another day. If you have self-doubt, remember that you never really lose...you either win or you learn from the experience.

BUILD SELF-ESTEEM

At times, we all suffer from insecurity that weakens us and prevents us from achieving our highest potential and reaching our greatest goals. This is a normal human trait, fueled by fear, which can often lead to failure. While we have discussed that knowledge is the best antidote, it is important to understand why. When you are armed with information, you'll find yourself extraordinarily well positioned to feel a sense of confidence in all that you do. Confidence, then, can propel you ahead and even closer to your dreams. Likely, you can think of many people who portray confidence in all that they do. "It is easy for them," you may mumble under your breath. But they are the best because they are confident, not the other way around.

The word "confidence" comes from the Latin word *fidere*, which means to trust. Having confidence, therefore, is to trust yourself to succeed and make the right choices that support your future needs and wants. The more confident we are, the greater likelihood that we will successfully execute our goals. However, the other side of the coin is also true. Lacking confidence will make you hold back, rarely take chances, and avoid risk for fear of failure. So then, where does inner confidence originate? It begins with self-esteem, a prerequisite to having confidence. Self-esteem and self-confidence are directly related. Both have a high correlation to academic performance and overall positive mental health. People will treat you the way you treat yourself, reinforcing and compounding your basic insecurity. Perception, therefore, becomes reality.

We all know the Golden Rule, to treat *others* the way you wish to be treated *yourself*. In addition to the Golden Rule, perhaps we should establish a Platinum Rule. In other words, if you treat *yourself* the way you want to be treated by *others* then you will indelibly hold yourself to a higher standard. This will manifest itself in a higher self-confidence that will, in turn, encourage others to believe in you. It can literally impact everything that you do. It has been said that how you do anything is how you do everything, and if you apply confidence to your everyday behavior, you will certainly achieve something special in your life. This will produce a virtuous cycle of hope, replacing the negative cycle of despair. Rarely then will we accept anything less than the best we must give. In doing so, we are not just confident, we are ready. We are ready to "win."

PREPARE TO WIN

Harvey Mackay, business guru and author of *Swim With The Sharks Without Being Eaten Alive*, who was previously mentioned in this book, is also a member of the Horatio Alger Association of Distinguished Americans. Riding together to an event in Washington, DC, I told Harvey about my plans to write this book. He leaned over and whispered some great advice. He said that it would be easy for him to distill all the advice he's provided in his seven *New York Times* best-selling books in just three words. The advice, he said, applies to every student, every businessperson, every athlete, and everyone who wants to succeed in anything they do, big or small. The three words, he said, are "prepare to win." I had to ask him to repeat it. Then it hit me. Prepare, and you will win. Preparation is what it takes to win...in school, in business, and, of course, in life. "This is my gift to you," he said with a smile. "Prepare to win. Share that advice with your readers, and they will come away richer for this simple but powerful truth."

He continued, "Preparation will give you the confidence to accomplish anything you set your mind to. Self-confidence is highly correlated to academic success, but it is equally important in all aspects of life. Self-confidence is not just a state of mind, it requires proactive behavior. Specifically, it requires preparation. Preparation breeds confidence, and confidence breeds success." His words overwhelmed me. I hadn't expected such a pivotal conversation to have occurred in that car, but I was grateful for the advice.

The Roman philosopher Seneca is known for saying, "Luck is what happens when preparation meets opportunity." This quote reminds us that we make our own luck. The difference between lucky and unlucky people, we have seen before, is all in our perspective. It is in how we prepare each day of our lives. Lucky people generate their own good fortune via four basic principles:

1. They believe in themselves.
2. They listen to their intuition.
3. They have positive expectations.
4. They adopt a resilient attitude that transforms bad luck into good luck.

This creates a self-fulfilling prophecy of success. A profound example of "preparation meeting opportunity" is the professional career of NFL quarterback Tom Brady. A reporter once asked Brady if he still gets nervous before games. His answer may surprise you, but it is typical Brady, nonetheless. He said he does get nervous, but not on game day. He is most nervous when the team first starts practicing during the week. As the week goes on and he studies game tapes and learns about his opponent, he gains confidence and loses any sense of unrest.

Preparation equals confidence. Tom Brady's preparation allows him to anticipate what he will see and to plan his game-time strategy well in advance of the game, and this translates into confidence. A favorite Brady story comes from New England Patriots owner Robert Kraft. Soon after the Patriots drafted him, Brady walked up to Kraft and said, "I'm Tom Brady." Kraft replied, "I know who you are. You are our sixth-round draft pick." Kraft recalled Brady looking him in the eyes and saying, "That is right. And I am the best decision this organization has ever made!" Preparation is just one of the traits Brady uses to build his confidence.

Several other traits that are evident in the greatest professional athletes, like Tom Brady or Michael Jordan, who exhibit relentless confidence include:

> *Desire*: Brady does not just prepare to win, he "wants" to win. That translates into a "whatever it takes" attitude. After setting passing records in the Monday night game, he can be found watching game tapes of next week's opponents to prepare. Now that is motivation! It is desire that supports the confidence that is so essential to a successful outcome. Whether the game of football or the game of life, one must have a desire to succeed for confidence to prevail.

Emotion: Brady brings a passion to the field. He brings an infectious love for the game that everyone around him can feel. He has intense emotion when he plays. The key is to channel that emotion into a positive energy that makes us confident and not self-destructive. On the playing field or in the boardroom, we can see emotion play out in both positive and negative ways. *Golf Magazine* interviewed Masters champion Jon Rahm following his 2023 Masters victory. He explained his success in managing negative emotion after a disappointing finish the week before. When asked how he put those thoughts aside to win the 2023 Masters Tournament, he quoted the popular show Ted Lasso and said, "Be a goldfish. You know why? He's got a ten-second memory. I played great golf last week, just a couple bad swings down the stretch, and that's the most important thing to remember." Rahm was able to manage negative thoughts and channeled his emotion into positivity, a confidence that was apparent in every swing during his successful Master's victory.

Learning from Failure: Tom Brady didn't complete every single pass, didn't win every game, and didn't end every season hoisting up the Lombardi Trophy after winning the Super Bowl. Dealing with failure is an essential element of confidence...and of success. Another "greatest" of his sport, Michael Jordan, talks about his "misses" all the time. "I've missed over 9,000 shots in my career," he said. "I have lost almost 300 games. Twenty-six times I have been trusted to take the game winning shot and missed. I have failed

> over and over and over again in my life. And that is why I succeed."

The strength of desire, emotion, and the ability to learn from failure are evident in the most successful athletes and the most successful individuals in virtually any endeavor. They learn from their success and they learn from their mistakes. These same fundamentals apply to us all. In short, to have the confidence you need to succeed, you should emulate the process of an elite athlete who radiates confidence in front of the cameras and behind them. They set the tone for the team both on the practice field and in training. They prepare at an elite level, and this pushes their teammates to improve individually and as a group. With confidence, we can be the quarterbacks (or coaches) of our own lives!

THE HALLMARK OF TRUE CONFIDENCE IS HUMILITY

One of the many challenges of those with confidence is to prevent others from perceiving that confidence as a false pretense or even arrogance. There is a fine line between confidence and arrogance that we all must traverse. Former President Donald Trump is, in many ways, a personification of confidence. But while navigating the fine line between confidence and arrogance, it could be said that he knows no line and is often accused of being overconfident and self-serving. Trump learned his confidence from his father Fred's obsession with famous 1950s self-help author Norman Vincent Peale.

Peale was a minister who preached self-confidence. He wrote a bestselling self-help book called *The Power of Positive Thinking* in 1952, which has provided a road map to success to many. Peale was also one of the founders of the Horatio Alger Association. He wrote, "Obstacles are simply not permitted to destroy your happiness and well-being. You need be defeated only if you are willing to be... Believe in yourself! Have faith in your abilities! Without a humble but reasonable confidence in your own powers, you cannot be successful or happy." In this advice, the word "humble" is a critical force.

If Peale were alive today, he might have counseled the former president on the importance of humility. In that delicate balance between confidence and humility, we must recognize that a line does exist that we cannot cross. When confidence turns into abject arrogance, it can also defeat us. Humility is sometimes seen as a sign of low self-regard. That is hardly the case. Quite the opposite is true. The best of us are the humblest among us. Humility is the recognition that we should be grateful for what we have accomplished. It is the practice of recognizing that there is always more to do. Humility comes from our acceptance that personal greatness does not come at the expense of others but because of others. It helps us deal with change and turn failure into knowledge without letting it defeat us. Humility accentuates the difference between confidence and arrogance. It is having enough confidence or self-esteem to know that you don't need to brag or flaunt your greatness. It is the self-awareness to know that you always have room for improvement.

A few years ago, I invited General Charles Duke to a dinner at The Cooper Institute in Dallas. Charlie was an Air Force fighter pilot and the lunar module pilot of Apollo 16. He was the tenth person to walk on the moon. The speaker for the evening was Admiral William McRaven, former Navy Seal and ninth commander of the US Special Operations Command. Charlie was seated between Admiral McRaven and Roger Staubach, Hall of Fame Dallas Cowboys quarterback and one of the best to ever play the game. All three of these great men were graduates of the Naval Academy. During the dinner, Admiral McRaven started small talk with Charlie Duke. After learning that he was a fellow graduate of the Naval Academy and a former Air Force pilot, he didn't ask any further questions about General Duke's background, making small talk for the rest of the dinner.

When dinner concluded, Roger turned to Admiral McRaven and said, "Wasn't it great to chat with Charlie Duke?" The Admiral said,

"Yes, Roger, but he didn't say much. What did he do after leaving the Academy?" Roger laughed and said, "That's Charlie Duke of Apollo 16. He's one of four men alive who have walked on the surface of the moon." The admiral was floored. Throughout dinner, he was unaware and, of course, Charlie was not one to brag. Shortly after the dinner, McRaven wrote a book called *The Hero Code: Lessons Learned from Lives Well Lived.* He devoted an entire chapter of the book to "humility," one of the traits highlighted in the Hero Code. He referred to his dinner with Charlie Duke to illustrate his point.

BEWARE OF THE CONFIDENCE KILLERS

Much of what happens to us is out of our immediate control. That is not to say we cannot control our destiny, but there are times when it may feel as though everyone is working against us. Negativity, especially the negative attitudes of those around us, is one of the worst enemies of confidence. Too often, we are surrounded by others who not only lack confidence but whose negativity then becomes yet another hill we must climb. It stacks the deck against us. Naysayers, jealousy, and mediocrity among our peers can be a cancer that slowly eats away at our confidence and may erode our success.

What happens to the child who raises his hand in class? Often, his peers tease or ridicule him. Perhaps he is called a teacher's pet or even bullied, resulting in a hit to self-confidence that could be a one-time thing or a lasting blow to self-esteem. A debilitating herd mentality can occur in groups. The same phenomenon can occur in the classroom, the workplace, or the playing field. Others may see our hard work as a threat. This, of course, is rooted in fear. "By raising your hand, you make me look bad, so I will discourage you from such behavior" is the unspoken but palpable threat. Since human nature may cause many to look for the easy path, they may have an inclination or desire to work as little as possible. As a result, each of us may be pressured to "conform" or to retreat to the middle of the pack. Unfortunately, this is a herd-like behavior that discourages outliers and individual performance.

As a high school student, I took a summer job in the factory where my father once worked. He often said he did not want me to work there, that he wanted me to have a better life with "freedom." At the time, I did not understand. I thought the factory work looked like fun, so I tried it out for a summer, cutting large abrasive blocks into small blocks on a large and dangerous machine.

I soon became proficient and discovered that "piece work" provided an incentive, allowing me to make more money for each block I produced. I began to work harder and harder, proud of my success. Before long, a fellow worker counseled me to take my time and slow down. I listened to his advice but never lost the desire to make more money to put toward my college tuition. Before long, the counsel turned into a threat and then devolved into violence. I found myself in an old-fashioned brawl. What started as an effort to deflect his punches ended up with the two of us surrounded by a cheering (or jeering) crowd. A few moments later I was in the general manager's office trying to explain my behavior. "Your father worked here for many years," he said, "and never caused moment of trouble. You have been here for two weeks and start a fight?"

I was mortified. I tried to explain but the general manager was having none of it. In my zeal for success, I was hurting the "scale" and inadvertently putting everyone at jeopardy of having to work harder because I was raising the expectation of what could and should be produced per hour. Even the boss explained that this was the "system," and they had no intention of letting some ambitious kid mess up the "system." I suddenly understood my father's frustration with the factory and how he faced limitations of his own freedom, including his freedom to make more money on the job. I also understood my father's admonition to choose a better life. Still, I was grateful for the lesson. This scenario plays out every day in the classroom and the workplace.

The outlier is often discouraged, threatened, or even bullied to conform. It is an attack on self-confidence and a threat to individual success. In some cases, such behaviors are systemic and unavoidable. This is not a behavior limited to hourly roles. When taking my first job in a white-collar environment, I discovered the same forces at work. During a summer internship while at graduate school, my fellow professionals "counseled" me. "You're working too hard," they said. Maybe you should take it easy and enjoy your summer." Meanwhile, they were concerned that the summer help would make them look bad. The irrational fear among others that your work will diminish the importance of theirs can be present in any environment. Whether on the job or in the classroom, the behaviors are the same and can crush one's self-confidence and/or desire to succeed... but only if we allow it to happen.

The mock-Latin expression *Illegitimi non carborundum* ("Don't let the bastards grind you down") conveys the point quite well. I adopted it as a sticker for my high school notebook as a reminder to stay the course and not to let others, out of jealousy or fear, determine my destiny. The phrase originated during World War II. Lexicographer Eric Partridge attributes it to British army intelligence early in the war. It means that the fear and lack of confidence in both yourself and others can pull you down. In those cases, it is best to move on to another opportunity. In *no* case, however, should this circumstance be allowed to diminish one's confidence.

Confidence comes in many shapes and sizes. American Red Cross chairman and Horatio Alger recipient Bonnie McElveen-Hunter tells the story of her mother, Madeline, taking her and her sister to the backyard, making them write "can't" on a piece of paper and then burying that word in a box underground...never to be used again. It worked. McElveen-Hunter rose from childhood adversity to become a successful entrepreneur, owner of Pace Communications, ambassador to Finland, and the longest-tenured chairman of the American Red Cross. She became CEO of her own life at an early age, recognizing that change equals opportunity. McElveen-Hunter is rich by many standards, but her richness is not about wealth. She is rich in character. She enjoys the freedom to move in any circle, from handing out blankets and water in a natural disaster to hosting the elegant International Red Cross Ball in Palm Beach. She is rich in freedom!

An interesting sub note is that McElveen-Hunter works harder than most people we know. She manages a full-time professional career as chief executive of her own company in addition to working in her second full-time role as American Red Cross chairman, regularly putting in twelve- to eighteen-hours days and seven-day workweeks. With all this freedom and wealth, why does she work so hard?

To McElveen-Hunter, and others who have become the CEOs of their lives, this is not "work," it is an expression of freedom to do what they enjoy doing most. If you enjoy your work, then it is not working in the traditional sense. McElveen-Hunter does not have to work. She could spend the years that most would define as a time of retirement by enjoying the fruits of her labor. She is certainly free to do that. Freedom, to her, is about doing those things that give her enjoyment, whether "working" or relaxing at a cafe in Paris. She is free to control her own destiny. She has made change a constant in her life. She refuses to allow the word "can't" to influence her in any way. She is not alone. You may then wonder exactly how people like McElveen-Hunter seem to rise to the top and succeed despite great challenges and change. They do this through knowledge, determination, and, of course, education. These are the common denominators we often see.

You too can become a winner and a lifelong learner. Very simply, the more you know the more confident you will be. The more confidence you have, the more freedom you will enjoy. It is clear, the more you believe in yourself, the more adept you will be at reaching your goals. Confidence must come from inside. Once you bury "can't" in a box in the backyard, develop your self-confidence, and use it in a humble way, your trajectory will be to "infinity and beyond"!

CHAPTER 7

CLARITY: KEEP IT SIMPLE...SMART!

"Simplicity is the ultimate sophistication."

Leonardo da Vinci

It is not always easy to see the road ahead. At times, you will be navigating in darkness without certainty of direction. A pilot must learn to fly in the clouds without visual reference, relying only on instrumentation and data to fly safely. The data from his instruments provides guidance. That is the light shining in the darkness. Even with uncertainty, we still have control over our actions and outcomes. It is our search for understanding, for light in the darkness, that leads to clarity. With clarity, we become empowered to see the light and shine the light, two qualities that offer tremendous insight into the future. Yes, we can fly in the dark.

Defined as the quality of being coherent and intelligible, clarity is fundamental to communication. In turn, communication is fundamental to both teaching and learning. Still, we often complicate, obfuscate, confuse, and muddle even the simplest of concepts. Why? It is sometimes inadvertent. Sometimes we lack complete understanding of a concept, inevitably causing confusion. Other times, we may be acquiring too much knowledge resulting in an overload of information. In either case, we can confound both inbound and outbound communication resulting in confusion.

Clarity is an art form grounded in simplicity. How ironic that most of us find simplicity to be such a difficult task. As famously noted by Albert Einstein, "If you can't explain it to a six-year-old, you don't understand it yourself." Einstein wasn't trying to be sarcastic. He was aiming to demonstrate that the better we understand a topic, the greater control we will have with the use of that information. We've all heard the expression K.I.S.S. (Keep it Simple, Stupid). I prefer to use a small variation...Keep it Simple, Smart! As mentioned in the last chapter, we sometimes learn more from our losses than from our wins. If I reflect on my Blockbuster experience, improved clarity is one element that could have helped the business survive despite the economic challenges we faced.

Our vision was to make Blockbuster the aggregator of all streaming content including new releases, older movies, foreign films, television, and more. Just as it was in physical stores, our online business was to the be one-stop shop for convenient access to media content. We would use the physical stores to transition to that model over time, ultimately helping customers make the smooth transition to streaming and slowly closing stores as the format shifted. While that transition occurred, we would provide *Total Access*, by making it convenient for customers to find their favorite movie via in-store, by-mail, via kiosk, or through Blockbuster On Demand. This approach was not unlike the transition made when customers shifted from VHS to DVD. Blockbuster was able to adapt to that change in format and helped its customers facilitate that transition.

The long-term strategic plan for the future of Blockbuster was clear in my mind. It wasn't clear to others, including some of the most senior members of my management team. We had a straightforward plan—to manage the stores as profitably as possible while migrating the business to a digital platform. Our challenge, at the time, was to make Blockbuster On Demand available on all electronic devices. Televisions during that period were not "smart" or connected, the iPhone was just recently released, and the iPad was not yet in the market. The ubiquitous "apps" that we take for granted today were just beginning to emerge. Consumer electronics manufacturers were reluctant to build applications into their devices to make it easier to order Netflix or Blockbuster On Demand, so most of the streaming was being done by kids on their video game consoles at the time.

To accelerate the availability of Blockbuster On Demand, we decided to explore a merger with Circuit City, the one-time competitor of Best Buy stores. As the second largest electronics retailer in the U.S., they would have the power to require manufacturers of every cell phone, computer, or television include the Blockbuster app on all new devices. We could then offer Blockbuster On Demand to anyone buying a new television, phone, or computer. This would be the ultimate in convenient access to media entertainment. While this may have been a good "concept," the complexity of this transaction and the confusion it caused both internally and externally may have hurt our cause. Circuit City rebuffed our merger/acquisition offer and the attempt confused the investment community. They didn't see this move as a pathway to accelerate our digital offerings but instead thought we were going to double down on brick-and-mortar retail stores.

Despite my personal mantra regarding clarity and the importance of simplicity, I had violated my own rule and brought a significant amount of complexity to the equation. This was not adherence to the rule of "Keep it Simple"...and it wasn't "Smart." The degree of difficulty to execute this strategy caused unnecessary confusion and distraction at a time when we needed to remain focused on the financial challenges. The move didn't kill Blockbuster's ultimate chances of success, but it certainly made the hill more difficult to climb once the financial crisis hit. Could I have chosen a more effective plan? Yes, if my listening skills were more in tune with what the investment community was telling me at the time.

CLARITY STARTS WITH LISTENING

Listening is a crucial practice to gain clarity and to literally "hear" the information you're receiving. It may sound simple to do, but how often does someone speak to us and we realize, after the fact, that we didn't understand a word? Consider this simple example: When someone introduces themselves, do you always hear their name? Did you make a conscious effort to listen to their name and make a further effort to commit it to memory? Too often we listen but we don't hear. We are unconsciously framing a response and are sometimes more worried about what we will say rather than what we hear. The result? We walk away and realize that we never actually "heard" the other person's name. And the next time we see them, we can't recall it.

Mark Cuban has shared an anecdote about clarity and listening. He said, "This guy who was trying to be my mentor [said], 'I'm going to give you a tool that you can use: Every time you go into a meeting, I want you to have a notepad, and the minute you sit down, I want you to write the word 'Listen' right there on your notepad. You need this because you do not listen.'" Since then, this is a habit that has stuck with Cuban. "No lie," Cuban said, "if you go back over the last forty years now that I have been going into meetings and taking notes, I write, 'Listen,' first thing." The ability to listen helped him learn, a skill that he attributes to his continued success. "I recognized that learning was truly a skill," Cuban told Men's Health in 2020, "and that by continuing to learn, to this day, I'm able to compete and keep up and get ahead of most people."[13]

This simple but valuable advice allowed him to focus and bring great clarity to understanding the situation because he was listening. Too often we get distracted and lose focus. Are we focused on the topic and receiving the information in a way that we can process

13 Taylor Locke, "Mark Cuban: The Advice I Got from a Mentor at 22 Years Old That I Still Use Today," CNBC, April 17, 2021, https://www.cnbc.com/2021/04/17/mark-cuban-advice-i-got-from-a-mentor-at-22-years-old-that-i-use.html.

and store? Or do we let the words wash over us like waves, realizing later that only a few of them remain in our consciousness? As Mark Cuban admits, effective listening is the key to learning.

I was once listening to a businessman named Dumas Siméus, CEO of a large supply company, speak about relationships and the importance of diversity. Following the speech, I approached Siméus to shake his hand. He surprised me by saying that he was grateful for my attention. He said, "You were one of very few in the audience of hundreds who had your antennae up."

I asked him to explain. A Haitian, Siméus is a very spiritual man who believes in the ability to connect with people on a higher level. He said that he finds most people have their antennae down. They are not in receiving mode and go through life letting words and ideas wash over them with little comprehension or interest. He then said only a select few are in receiving mode. Their antennae are up, and they are hearing more than just others' words. They are receiving the meaning, the intent, and the passion. Siméus said that they are giving and receiving the love for their fellow human being by being "in tune" with each other.

No one teaches us how to learn. From the time we are born we face a barrage of people teaching us things, but no one teaches us why we should learn or *how* we should learn. They just teach things, and we listen...sometimes. We end up on the receiving end. Go to school, get taught, go home and study, repeat.

It is like watching television in the old days with four channels. Turn it on, let it flow over us. We may only pay attention sometimes or just have the television on for background noise. Learning can be the same. Are we listening, or do we just let the teaching wash over us? Do we have the lessons on for background noise, or did we curate our learning to focus on this topic we wish (or need) to know? In either case, the decision must start from within...a curiosity about something, then a quest to seek it out. Each of these stories addresses "how" we are listening, but we should also consider "why" we listen.

THE IMPORTANCE OF UNDERSTANDING YOUR "WHY"

Nearly as important as listening to information is to also understand why we are listening to it. Consider algebra. If you are listening to an algebra lesson without asking why, there is a very low chance of clarity of communication or basic comprehension. Many of us make it through one or two years of high school algebra and perhaps a year or two in college without ever asking (or being told) the practical application of this tool and how it will affect us day to day.

Without understanding the why, it is difficult to have clarity around the subject at all. In addition, we may not even value it. It is just a topic we must study to meet our basic curriculum requirements. Learning becomes rote memorization of principles or rules rather than the application of those rules with clarity of purpose. The difference is huge and will make a significant impact on retention.

For example, have you ever explored the "why" behind learning mathematics? Have you considered the idea that learning math is like learning a language? Math is, indeed, a universal language shared by all cultures and across all spoken languages. The solution to a problem in algebra or a formula in trigonometry is the same in any corner of the globe. To learn basic communication in Japanese took years of study. To have become fluent in reading or writing Japanese would have taken even more intense learning. Mathematics isn't any different, but the investment of time is like learning a language that is universal in nature. Even if you don't plan to be a mathematician, an accountant, or even an economist to whom math will be a critical part of your career, the discipline of learning mathematics will make you a better learner and a better problem solver in any field.

Understanding means having the ability to change your perspective. The essence of mathematics is about finding patterns, or connections, rules that govern what we see. It is about making assumptions and playing with them to see what happens. Mathematics enables us to do many things. There are patterns in nature, music, dance, and art. Written language is a pattern. A barcode on your products in the grocery store represents a pattern. All computer coding is done with a series of patterns using 1 and 0.

Math is all around us in everything we see and do, from the symmetry of lines in nature to the hours and seconds in a day. Take the *golden ratio* as an example. In mathematics, this is the ratio of a line segment cut into two pieces of different lengths such that the ratio of the whole segment to that of the longer segment equals the ratio of the longer segment to the shorter segment. The origin of this number, which is approximately equal to 1.618, can be traced back to Ancient Greek mathematicians who first studied the ratio because of its common appearance in geometry. Euclid's *Elements* (c. 300 BC) provides several propositions and their proofs employing the golden ratio. You will see this ratio appear in everything from art (the proportions of the *Mona Lisa*) to architecture to the intricate structure of a leaf in nature.

Further, every algebraic equation is a metaphor for comparing things. It allows us to apply tools to solve a mathematical equation that produce different perspectives to produce the same result. When applied to non-math situations, the same approach can generate a higher level of understanding. Just as with a mathematical equation, changing one's perspective can create a higher level of understanding too. It is difficult to comprehend just how mathematics can contribute to improved understanding of a non-math problem, but solving equations is more than just solving for numbers, it is about rewiring your brain to approach problem-solving from a different perspective. Neil deGrasse Tyson, physicist and mathematician, puts the importance of learning math in simple terms in a National Geographic podcast called *StarTalk* where he talks about Debunking the "Pointless" Education Myth.

"People think that when they take math in school," he observes, "there's the common response like, 'I will never need to use this for the rest of my life,' as they learn trig identities, or the Pythagorean theorem, or whatever it is that we all remember learning, feeling pretty sure that it's never going to show up again." He notes, however, that we are missing something important with that way of thinking. "It misses the fact," he says, "that learning how to do the math establishes a new kind of brain wiring in your mind, a kind of problem-solving brain wiring. It's not about what you've learned, it's about what methods, tools, and tactics you had to develop in order to solve the problem that you may never see again for the rest of your life. But you will see other problems where these methods and tools will become immensely valuable to you." Neil deGrasse Tyson has a very practical approach to education. He worries less about how much information you pour into your head, and more about how equipped you are to use it to explore the world around you.

COMMUNICATION CLARITY: INBOUND AND OUTBOUND CLARITY

You should always consider your effectiveness in delivering a message. How a speaker or leader delivers a message is just as important as the message they impart. Learning requires more than just receiving information. Effective learning also requires giving information. Two types of clarity impact the overall effectiveness of your message: inbound clarity and outbound clarity. They are quite unique in their own ways and have their special impact on how we understand our world. Inbound clarity is a process of listening, comprehending, validating, and evaluating. Outbound clarity is communicating, teaching, persuading, and presenting facts.

Inbound clarity may be exemplified in the use of the Socratic method, a form of learning dialogue between individuals. The Greek philosopher Socrates used this approach to improve understanding.

The method searches for commonly held truths that make up one's beliefs and challenges them to determine their consistency with one's other beliefs. It is basically the process of asking and answering questions to stimulate critical thought and draw out ideas and concepts in simple form. Every law school across the United States teaches this method. It is a highly effective way to create inbound clarity. More about Socratic reasoning when we address it in the next chapter on Critical Thinking. Inbound clarity is ultimately the ability to listen *and* comprehend.

Next is outbound clarity, or the art of communicating our findings and conclusions to others. Clear communication involves efficient and streamlined messaging. If an organization doesn't understand a strategy or specific tactics, it will not properly execute it and will likely fail in its endeavors. Everyone in the organization must understand the plan and do their part to execute the strategy. It requires effective communication.

This communication process can be like a game of telephone played by children at camp while sitting around a campfire. In the game, one child turns to the friend to their left or right and whispers a secret in their ear. That person tells the next and the next until the secret makes its way around the circle back to the original child. When the last person shares the secret out loud, the whole group generally breaks into laughter to hear how a simple message became so wildly misinterpreted after making its way around the entire group.

This same process occurs in every business every day. Imagine a company like 7-Eleven or Blockbuster with at least ten layers of management between the CEO and a store manager or franchisee. The CEO may set out a strategy and expect that it will be carried out by the team and accomplished at each store. Meanwhile, that direction is communicated from person to person through ten layers of management with the resulting execution sometimes bearing little resemblance to the original plan. This is the same result as the telephone game, but in a corporate environment, the results could be devastating.

To improve company-wide communications, I took a page from Sam Walton's playbook at Walmart. The founder of Walmart once fought this communications problem by pulling all field managers into their Bentonville, Arkansas, headquarters for a weekly Saturday sales meeting. This way, the field organization could hear Walton directly explain his strategy and outline the team's priorities for the week. I adopted a similar approach using telecommunications to link everyone in the company for a weekly message. In that meeting, I would identify three priorities for each week around which everyone in the organization could align. The result was greater clarity of communications and dramatically improved execution. When at the helm of both 7-Eleven and Blockbuster, I used telecommunication links to accomplish this same direct line of communication with the field, holding weekly video communications meetings with the entire organization.

That's the thing about clear communication—it is only as good as the last person who receives the message. If you create a pure message, which then gets diluted over time and from person to person, ear to ear, you will hardly have your original intention in place. This is why it is important not just to deliver an effective message but to deliver it effectively. Make no mistake, that is not always easy. And as you begin to factor in how different people receive and understand messages, it certainly doesn't make it easier.

Both inbound clarity (listening, critical thinking, and understanding) and outbound clarity (the ability to communicate effectively and persuade others to follow your lead) require knowledge. This is where education comes into play. The more we know about what we want to communicate and how we choose to communicate it, the better. Then, it is crucial that we carefully curate the message and deliver it to our intended audience. While not always easy to execute, it is at the center of our institutional learning and education process. Think of a classroom teacher who has an intimate and familiar knowledge of the course content. That teacher will be successful because of his or her vast familiarity of the topic but also in how they deliver it to the students. Keep it simple, *smart*!

Simplicity is a constant learning process that we must practice daily. The more we communicate with clarity, the more we learn; and the more we learn, the more effective our communication will be. The more we can break complex problems into their simple components, the better our understanding; therefore, the more effectively we will make decisions. In both cases, we have a virtuous cycle of learning that can lead to personal growth. Whether listening, learning, or leading a team, message clarity is an essential element to successful communication. Taking the complex and breaking it down into simple terms is the secret sauce of all learning. Just as Albert Einstein taught us, true genius is taking the complex and making it simple.

SECTION III
HOW TO LEARN

Now that we know *what* to learn, as in the importance of embracing change, having confidence, and demonstrating the ability to have clarity of thought and communications, we can focus on *how* to learn.

- **Critical Thinking:** The ability to discern fact from fiction is a fundamental part of our learning process. I like to consider critical thinking as the algebra of thought because it is the fundamental process of breaking down problems into their components and solving them based on the available data. Only then can we determine what is true or false, enabling us to make the best decision with the information available.
- **Curiosity:** Intellectual curiosity is the root of all knowledge. There are two kinds of learners; the first are the curious ones, who are proactive and always asking questions. The second type, those that are reactive, remember only information they find relevant. An essential element to developing solutions and a fundamental piece of the learning puzzle is the ability to understand all sides of an issue. The more curious we are, the more we will traverse life in a meaningful and connected way.
- **Creativity:** We are all born creative. For success, it is essential to nurture that creativity and to stimulate the right brain. We can all develop our own creative side, if only given the chance and encouraged to do so. The creative mind also allows for greater freedom to think without being encumbered by predisposed rules and boundaries, very simply, to have fun!

While there are certainly more steps in "How" to learn, we have focused on the three most critical elements to enable your intellectual growth. This, of course, assumes that the learning fundamentals of reading, writing, and basic arithmetic are in place. It is not learning alone that matters, but the relevance of that learning to our continued growth. This is where critical thinking, curiosity, and creativity come into play. It is not just what you learn but how you put that learning into play in solving problems, whether a mathematical equation, a scientific discovery, or a simple business solution. It is your ability to ask why, to walk through a process of analysis, to use data to make informed decisions, to dig deeper for more insight, and to have the creativity to explore new hypotheses. These three tools, *critical thinking, curiosity,* and *creativity,* will help you realize "How" to learn, an essential step for your educational journey.

CHAPTER 8

CRITICAL THINKING: UNDERSTANDING YOUR "WHY"

"It is the mark of an educated mind to be able to entertain a thought without accepting it."

Aristotle

Critical thinking is one of the more essential skills needed to navigate the modern world. The ability to think critically is a prerequisite to making informed decisions. With an abundance of information and media surrounding us twenty-four seven, it is easy to let others do the thinking on our behalf. If we do, we allow others to form our opinions, determine our allegiances and even shape our character. Instead, it is essential that we understand the importance of thinking for ourselves, asking the right questions, and doing the research necessary to determine truth from conjecture.

At its core, critical thinking is the process of analyzing information, evaluating evidence, and making reasoned judgments. It is the intellectual embodiment of the scientific method itself. We establish a hypothesis or a point of view. We then gather information or do our own research and determine our course of action. We then take a specific action, whether we choose to cast a vote for our preferred candidate or take a political stance that is based on our own belief system. We can then measure the success of that action against our expected results.

After measuring the results of our actions, we can remain open to new information that may cause us to modify our hypothesis and perhaps cause us to create a new action or conclusion. This iterative process of asking questions, examining assumptions, weighing evidence, and arriving at informed conclusions is the essence of critical thinking. This is the inverse of "reactive" thinking. Instead, it is proactive in nature, a deliberate process that requires focus, discipline, and a willingness to challenge one's own beliefs and assumptions.

Some of the earliest recorded examples of critical thinking are recorded in the teaching of Socrates, the Greek philosopher who lived in Athens between 470 and 399 BC. Socrates believed that we should always challenge those in authority because those in power are sometimes irrational or motivated by self-interest. Therefore, he encouraged his students to have an "interrogative soul." He established the importance of asking deep questions that probe into others thinking and intent before acceptance of others' ideas. This approach would serve us well in these days of social media and partisan news channels.

Socrates emphasized the importance of finding evidence, closely examining reasoning and assumptions, analyzing others' intentions, and exploring the implications of any one conclusion. His approach is called "Socratic questioning" and is the most widely known method of teaching critical thinking. In his line of questioning, Socrates would highlight the importance of clarity and consistency. He would easily expose others' irrational thinking or lack of information.

In his time in Ancient Greece, Socrates proved that authority does not always equate to factual knowledge. Another Greek Philosopher, Plato, recorded Socrates's teachings and furthered the teaching of critical thinking. Aristotle, and other later Greek scholars, would ultimately refine and expand on the teaching of Socrates eventually leading to our modern education processes and the teaching of critical thinking in our schools.

The root of Socratic reasoning is in his love for rational thinking. The field of logic is basically the analysis of arguments including an assessment of the accuracy or integrity of an argument. Critical thinking is "logically" correct, which allows for identification of logically true and logically false statements.

To understand this process, we must understand the three basic steps that encompass logical reasoning: deduction, induction, and abduction. Deduction is drawing a conclusion based on the facts that are at hand. Induction includes the critical thinking skills necessary to draw conclusion based on generalization. You put together pieces of information to draw the best conclusion based on the information at hand. Abduction takes critical thinking to another level. It is the ability to draw a conclusion based on the limited knowledge that you have, allowing you to think critically and make an educated guess. The fundamental benefit of critical thinking is our ability to enhance decision making. By analyzing information carefully and evaluating evidence objectively, critical thinkers are capable of better decision making, especially in complex or ambiguous situations. This can be particularly valuable in fields like business, healthcare, law, and education, where decisions can have far-reaching consequences.

An influential experience of my own educational journey was my participation in a "debate club." Anticipating a potential career as a lawyer, I envisioned myself as a young attorney arguing a case before the Supreme Court. Instead, I was a student, facing off against another student. The most meaningful part of the exercise was the practice of switching sides. In other words, each of us was required to argue the "other" side of a case to give us the experience of seeing and having to prepare arguments for and against the issue at hand. This, of course, required critical thinking and an ability to understand all sides of any given issue. The process contributed to the development of effective communication skills because by carefully analyzing facts, evidence, and assumptions, one becomes better able to articulate original ideas and engage in constructive dialogue with others.

Critical thinking is important for more than just debate. It can help individuals become more engaged and active citizens. By analyzing information carefully, evaluating evidence objectively, and making informed decisions, critical thinkers are better able to participate in the democratic process and make a positive impact on their communities. Some basic reasons for each of us to practice critical thinking are as follows:

> *Encourages independent thinking*: It is essential for all of us to independently develop our own ideas and opinions based on available data, evidence, and logic. It is all too easy to be swept into "groupthink" or to be swayed by what we see in social media or in the press. This is clearly relevant in society today where the massive amount of information available to us makes it easy to slip into our own communications bubbles, gathering only the information that supports our point of view. Independent thinking requires an understanding and assessment of every point of view.
>
> *Develops analytical skills*: Critical thinking is like math for words. The ability to solve complex problems comes down to breaking the problem into its components, then using information and available data to develop solutions for each piece of the problem, ultimately solving for the whole.
>
> *Improves decision making*: Once we can use analytical skills to solve for problems, decision making becomes easier. We can decide based on facts rather than intuition. We can be less vulnerable to being influenced by the bias of others.
>
> *Fosters academic success*: Critical thinking is different from simple "learning." It takes learning to a different level by assimilating learned information and adding elements of

deduction and induction to develop a point of view. Critical thinking is what we aspire to achieve from the educational process.

Facilitates "discernment": Our ability to make effective decisions depends on adequate collection of data, facts, figures, and all the information necessary to decide. Data, however, is never complete. Facts are sometimes falsehoods, and figures can sometimes lie. How, then, does one make a proper decision or develop a point of view with incomplete information? This is where judgement comes into play. Discernment is the ability to exercise judgement based on the best information available.

THE SCIENTIFIC METHOD

My Japanese partners at 7-Eleven reintroduced me to another form of critical thinking. When 7-Eleven expanded into the Japanese marketplace in the early 1970s, it began an entirely new approach to convenience retail. Because of the challenges of population density and small locations, Japan's 7-Eleven licensee was required to reinvent the convenience business. Little did we know that, many years later, the company that was founded in the U.S. would "re-learn" convenience retail from its most successful licensee in Japan.

During my first trip to visit the Japanese 7-Eleven store, I was amazed at their success. They had effectively used technology to reconstruct the entire supply chain to produce high quality fresh foods, yes even sushi, that was delivered three times per day at a cost lower than our once per week delivery to stores in the U.S. The remarkable success of these stores, using technology to provide enhanced decision-making tools yet unseen in U.S. retail, made me an eager student of their business model. I was also surprised by what I learned about their decision-making process. The Japanese have attributed much of their methodology and resulting success in business to an American named W. Edwards Deming. Deming is known as the father of the quality movement. Assigned to help the Japanese as part of the Marshall Plan following WWII, Deming was highly influential in post-WWII Japan.

As I learned the approach of my Japanese business partners, they shared a technique of critical thinking that seemed very familiar to me. It was roughly and somewhat simplistically translated from Japanese as "Plan, Do, See." It was part of Edward Deming's teachings in Japan. Basically, it is a variation of the scientific method we learned in grade school. We were taught to establish a *Plan* (an idea or hypothesis), to *Do* something (or put an action in place), to then *See* (measure or check) the results, then repeat the cycle. This same process is at the heart of the Japanese concept called "Kaizen" or continuous improvement. It resulted in dramatic improvement in Japanese business success worldwide. It also contributed to the success of 7-Eleven. When you buy your next Slurpee, simply look around the store and you'll find many products that are there because of the Plan, Do, See approach to critical thinking and decision making.

Even the 7-Eleven Slurpee was able to be improved using that approach. One of the perks of the chief executive role at 7-Eleven was a Slurpee machine in my office, for new product *testing* of course! For many years, I enjoyed Slurpees without thinking about the sugar content until one day, I asked how many calories were in each cup. Realizing that I was consuming several thousand calories per day from my favorite frozen beverage, I turned to the company's product development partners like Coke and Pepsi to request their help in formulating a low-calorie frozen carbonated beverage. Both companies accepted the challenge, but after several years of development effort, both had fallen short of the goal. The *hypothesis* was that a low-calorie frozen treat would be highly popular with both moms and the rest of us who wanted the indulgence without the guilt. The *plan* involved much more sophisticated scientific development than we ever anticipated. The challenge in reducing calories in such products is that sugar is an essential ingredient in the ability to achieve the semi-frozen state of the Slurpee drink. The scientists set out to develop an alternative to sugar that would produce the desired consistency and flavor. Neither Coca Cola nor Pepsi were successful at first. It was Kraft that ultimately created the first frozen carbonated breakthrough with their Crystal Light product. We then set out to accomplish the *do* step by working with Kraft to launch a Crystal Light Slurpee and to test the results. The next step was to *see* the results and to measure consumer response. Our customers loved the product as evidenced and measured by immediate sales success. The next step was then to repeat the cycle, expanding the plan to include Diet Coke Slurpee in the mix after they finally were able to develop their own formula. This cycle of continuous improvement continues today to create new products and flavors to delight the customer.

What makes the scientific method so unique is the critically important step of using data to measure results. Only by measuring results and modifying behavior can we achieve continuous improvement. This applies to all aspects of education and learning. Beyond education, it applies to all aspects of life. This simple method seeks clarity through a process of establishing a hypothesis, acting, measuring results, and then modifying our hypothesis and repeating the process, resulting in a virtuous cycle of continuous improvement. Following the method will bring clarity to virtually any decision-making process.

DEVELOPING GOOD "JUDGMENT"

Whether using the scientific method or any other approach to decision making, the basic definition of critical thinking is to analyze facts, data, and observations to form judgement. Noted scientist and astronomer Carl Sagan once noted that "knowing a great deal is not the same as being smart; intelligence is not information alone but also judgement, the manner in which information is collected and used."

Good judgement is one of those difficult concepts to define because it involves collecting input from many sources. Situational awareness, or an understanding of one's surroundings, will influence any information we may have. Cognitive ability, or the ability to analyze data effectively to determine an accurate result, is also an essential element. Finally, emotional intelligence is needed to avoid a "reactive" response that puts feelings over objectivity. With judgement we can make informed decisions that are based on the best information available without being influenced by emotion or nuance.

As we begin to understand our "why" and become more effective listeners, it is of great value to also determine what might otherwise impact our clarity. Discernment is one obstacle that impacts our ability to listen. How do we know if the information we are receiving is truthful or accurate? This is where critical thinking and intellectual curiosity become indispensable. The world is full of those communicating compelling information to us. That means that sometimes it can be a challenge to get a clear idea of the truth. In these days of an explosion of information via network, cable, streaming, or social media it is essential for us to be able to discern the difference between fact-checked news and political commentary. We must be able to separate fact from fiction, reasoning from rhetoric, and brilliance from BS. Again, we are often at risk of letting information flow over us without the critical thinking necessary to discern the real from the fake.

Compounding this challenge is the echo chamber effect of other voices joining in. In the case of the 2016 presidential campaign, for example, there were two pools of voices. Listening to CNN alone, one would believe that "building a wall" was a cruel and senseless act. Listening to Fox News alone, one would believe that all democrats wanted immigrants to flood the border to replace white, conservative voters. Both narratives were, to some degree, false and misleading. We sometimes forget that cable news channels are for-profit entities that thrive on ratings, naturally seeking to appeal to their target audience. The result can be like an echo chamber, which increases to a deafening volume when we are surrounded by like-minded friends or family who repeat the same narratives over and over until we are deafened by the sound of only one narrative in our ears...often dismissing the alternative as heretic or radical.

If the ability to determine truth was not difficult enough, we must be aware of the dangers of "false knowledge." As George Bernard Shaw said, "Beware of false knowledge. It is more dangerous than ignorance." The quote originated in Shaw's 1903 play *Man and Superman: A Comedy and a Philosophy*. In the play, a character named John Tanner is the author of a pamphlet entitled "The Revolutionist's Handbook." His "Maxims for Revolutionists" contains several short principles including: "Liberty means responsibility. That is why most men dread it." For a stable democracy to exist, voters must have knowledge and the ability to make informed decisions. Without education and continued learning, democracy will devolve into tribal camps fighting for their ideology but potentially oblivious to facts. The antidote is, of course, for everyone in a democracy to take responsibility for discernment of fact versus fiction. We must be able to separate political self-interest from policy implications on the whole of society. In turn, we must search for truth and truth requires knowledge. For a democracy to thrive, it requires a virtual cycle of continuous learning and truth seeking that will result in more effective governance for all. Education, in this context, is indeed Freedom!

In a democracy, therefore, each of us has a responsibility to use critical thinking. Certainly, your day-to-day responsibilities as a "listener" are hardly as complicated as when navigating election season. Nonetheless, the qualities you need to be successful as a voter during a heated election and as a student of life are the same. Critical thinking requires a dedicated effort to hear what people are saying, and to understand the world around you. Everyone's freedom of speech is memorialized in the Bill of Rights and the United States Constitution. Many will take advantage of that freedom for better or sometimes for worse. With modern technology giving everyone a vehicle to express that freedom, the ability to distinguish fact from fiction becomes exponentially more difficult. Freedom of speech puts even more pressure on the value of critical thinking. Access to more information requires us to curate that information to determine what is relevant and accurate. The question is...what do we do with that information? Our ability to use critical thinking to make informed decisions is sometimes a matter of survival for an individual or for humanity at large.

In the 1960s, during the Cold War, tensions between the United States and the Soviet Union were high. One day, a satellite detected a missile launch from the Soviet Union heading toward the United States. The military's early warning systems lit up, and they immediately alerted the President of the United States, John F. Kennedy, that the U.S. was under attack. Kennedy's advisors immediately urged him to launch a counterattack, but he hesitated. He knew that launching a counterattack could lead to a full-scale nuclear war, which would be catastrophic for both countries and the world. Instead of immediately responding to the situation, Kennedy asked his advisors to think critically about the situation and consider all possible options. He challenged them to gather more information and analyze the situation carefully before making any decisions. As it turned out, the missile launch was a false alarm caused by a malfunction in the satellite's system. If Kennedy had responded with a counterattack, it would have led to an all-out nuclear war, which would have had disastrous consequences.

This story reinforces the importance of critical thinking in government, especially in situations of crisis. Kennedy's ability to remain calm and weigh all the options before acting helped avert a potential disaster. It also highlights the importance of gathering accurate information, analyzing it carefully, and avoiding rash decisions based on incomplete information. Critical thinking is essential for leaders in politics to make wise and responsible decisions for the benefit of the nation and the world. Imagine the outcome of this situation or others that could have global implications if our leaders are not equipped with critical thinking skills. If they are influenced by emotion or unwilling to work toward fact-based decisions, the implications on humanity could be severe. Your informed decisions in the electoral process are more important than you may think.

So how does one practice critical thinking and put it to use every day? When it comes to academics, we should consider being proactive to both learn and practice critical thinking skills. Too often this is missing from today's curriculum. Rote memorization and the ability to pass multiple choice tests does not measure or teach the elements of critical thinking. Mathematics, for example, is mostly a practice of deductive reasoning in the form of mathematical proofs, but a student should be able to understand the difference between the deductive solutions to a mathematical model and the inductive reasoning in their science class.

All of this sounds tremendously complicated, especially for the student simply trying to learn. If we adhere to our own principles of clarity, we could break critical thinking into a very simple formula. For every decision, problem to be solved, or dilemma we face, we can use five simple questions to facilitate critical thinking and ultimately make better, more informed decisions:

Who: Who is involved in this decision? Who is providing the information? Who should be consulted? Who will be affected?

What: What are the facts available? What are the potential outcomes? What are the other perspectives?

Where: Where is the information sourced? Where can we get further data? Where are the areas of improvement?

When: When will the cost or benefit occur? When can we expect actions to be taken? When do we know we have succeeded?

Why: Why is this a problem or challenge to begin with? Why is it relevant to me or others? Why should we allow this to happen and why does it matter?

Armed with these simple questions, we can delve into any problem-solving scenario with a determination to gather the best available data, to separate fact from fiction, and to use the combination of deduction, induction, and abduction to determine the best possible answer or outcome with the information available. Driving this process requires diligence, but it has one other prerequisite need—curiosity.

CHAPTER 9

CURIOSITY: JET FUEL FOR LEARNING

"Non scholæ sed vitæ."

"We do not learn for school, but for life."

Lucius Annaeus Seneca

Intellectual curiosity is the root of all knowledge. It is the spark that kindled man's discovery of fire. It is the desire to investigate the unknown that inspired explorers to set out for the New World. It is the wonder of space that beckons us to search the far reaches of the universe. In essence, it is the spark that ignites our desire to learn. Curiosity is one of the more fundamental elements of learning. It represents the difference between rote memorization and understanding. It represents the difference between a teacher simply giving information and a student asking questions to better comprehend the information shared. It is the simple difference between receiving information versus a proactive giving and taking of knowledge.

In today's world, driven by rapid technological advancement and constant change, curiosity is an essential catalyst for personal growth and the ability to keep pace with change. It is the insatiable thirst for knowledge and the relentless pursuit of understanding that will contribute to progress for the individual and for society. It is only through curiosity that we can generate new ideas, challenge the assumptions of existing ideas, and ignite innovation. It is only thorough curiosity that humanity can progress while creating change for good.

Throughout history, there are countless examples of curiosity-driven innovation and change for the ultimate good of humanity. Going back thousands of years, early man demonstrated curiosity in solving fundamental practical problems of the day. Experimenting with materials and techniques, they crafted practical tools needed for survival. The ancient cave paintings demonstrate early man's curiosity and creativity in capturing the beauty of nature, animals, and the world around them.

It was curiosity about the world around them and the need to communicate with others that led to the development of early language. Beginning with symbols, sounds, and gestures to convey meaning, mankind was ultimately able to communicate within local groups. Looking beyond this world, the ancient civilizations such as Egyptians, Mayans, and Babylonians demonstrated a curiosity about the heavens. It was this quest for knowledge and keen observation that led to the development of calendars and ultimately led to advancements in mathematics and geometry. It was a curiosity about the night sky and the heavens above that led to celestial navigation, allowing mankind to explore the world.

This curiosity about the world and the practical need to navigate led the Chinese to invent the compass during the Han Dynasty, between 206 BC and 220 BC. This innovation allowed Chinese sailors to navigate great distances, resulting in exploration and trade. The Chinese are also credited with many innovations that accelerated the progress of humanity. Also during the Han Dynasty, the invention of paper making was credited to Cai Lin, whose curiosity and experimentation led to the creation of a practical writing surface, paper as we know it today. Imagine the power of this simple breakthrough on the progress of humanity by making written communications possible. It was not until the Song Dynasty (960–1279

BC) that the Chinese invented movable type printing, making book printing possible along with the dissemination of knowledge. It was Chinese alchemists, motivated by their desire to find an elixir for immortality, that caused them to discover the explosive properties of gunpowder. These examples highlight the Chinese people's historical contributions to science and technology. It also demonstrates the power of curiosity in advancing the progress of humanity and shaping the course of the future.

Curiosity has served as the accelerator for my own learning journey. I was fortunate to grow up in the dawn of space travel, watching with fascination as project Mercury, then Gemini, then Apollo took to the skies. Curiosity drives our exploration of space in the same way that explorers hundreds of years ago set out to explore the New World. Those intrepid explorers of the time, brave men like John Glenn, Buzz Aldrin, or Charlie Duke, were an inspiration for my own curiosity and desire to explore.

As NASA fueled my curiosity about space travel, I began to wonder how these rockets worked. I grew up within miles of the home of Robert Goddard, one of the pioneers of rocketry. If he could do it, so could I. My experimentation began with rocket propulsion, fashioning make-shift rockets out of the body of an old metal flashlight, adding external fins for stability, a nose cone to reduce drag, and a complex internal plastic bag (balloon) with a constrictor value (otherwise known as a small metal funnel) with gasoline as the only "rocket fuel" that I could access.

I was fortunate to avoid blowing myself up when the contraption failed to launch but instead set off a small explosion. Somewhat less fortunate was the vegetation burned down on a considerable plot of land. It was a hard lesson in failure, but it didn't quench my curiosity. Deciding that being a rocket scientist was probably not my calling, I shifted my curiosity to the inside of the spaceship and wanted to become an astronaut. Given the career path I've already described, it's clear that I fell short of that goal. My curiosity did, however, lead to the study of aviation and led me to pursue flying lessons at an early age. My early flying was based on the availability of funds, so it came a little slower than I had hoped but the curiosity and determination remained.

Each year, I train side by side with professional pilots in a flight simulator where my instructors throw every imaginable crisis at me. It is curiosity that drives me to understand the effects of wind-shear on the aircraft, to learn the latest technology for navigation, and to become an amateur meteorologist to understand weather patterns for safety in any conditions. It is curiosity that also drives my destinations, as I explore the world from the air. It is not only the destinations all over the world that stimulate that curiosity but the sights and sounds from above. Seeing the lights of a Starlink satellite train from forty thousand feet, the anvil cloud of a massive thunderstorm, or the amazing sight of a moonrise and sunset simultaneously viewed from each side of the cockpit are experiences and privileges driven by a curiosity that not only led to this aeronautical journey but propels it still today.

Curiosity makes the mind active. Curious people always ask questions and search for answers. Those who are not curious simply accept information as if they are a receptacle. An active mind is like any muscle—it becomes stronger through regular and repeated exercise. Exercising the mind through curiosity makes it stronger and sharper. In an article published in *Greater Good* magazine, Emily Campbell, PhD, wrote about six important attributes of curiosity. These include:

1. *Survival*: Curiosity increases our situational awareness, keeping us safe from danger. The urge to explore and inquire helps us be vigilant and gain knowledge about the constantly changing environment.

2. *Happiness*: The brain has been shown to release dopamine when we encounter new things. Curiosity has been shown

to be linked to higher levels of positive emotions, lower anxiety, and greater satisfaction.

3. *Achievement*: Curiosity has been measured to show a positive correlation to more active participation in school and higher academic achievement. It may seem like common sense, but when we are more curious about what we are doing, it becomes easier to become engaged.

4. *Empathy*: Curiosity about others makes us more aware of their lives and their opinions. When we are curious about other cultures and people unlike us, we learn about their unique qualities and become more empathetic toward them.

5. *Relationships*: One of the first principles of leadership development is for a leader to ask questions and to try to learn about the individuals on the team. Scientists call this approach "reciprocal self-disclosure." They discovered that people were seen as warmer and more attractive if they showed genuine curiosity in the other person. Demonstrating curiosity toward another is a great way to build your closeness with them.

6. *Health*: The curious know to be more inquisitive about their health and sensitive to those things that will favorably affect their well-being. Mental and physical health are favorably affected by curiosity.

Curiosity drives our desire to learn. As we learn more, we often increase our curiosity as well. It is a remarkable cycle, one that elevates each of us. The more curious we are, the greater understanding we will have of the world. The greater understanding we have of the world, the more opportunities we can seize and endeavors we can pursue.

The ability to be curious is ingrained in us from birth. It is not something acquired but rather something lost. That is, the older we get, the less it seems appropriate to explore and be creative in our daily lives. Sometimes, even the people we love can stifle our initial flame of curiosity, suggesting we fall into the societal norms and simply "stand in line." Sometimes complacency creeps in and replaces our curiosity. People lead us to believe that just accepting information is much better than challenging it, than asking questions to gain more insight around our clarity. Thomas Hobbes wrote, "Curiosity is the lust of the mind." Trust me when I say he was spot-on. The key to curiosity is to reawaken our passion for knowledge.

THE CURIOUS VERSUS THE COMPLACENT

There are two kinds of learners. The first is a curious, proactive individual who is always asking questions of the world around them. The second type of learner, a far cry from the first, is complacent and reactive; they allow information to flow over them, remembering only the things they find relevant. The history books quickly forget about the complacent. Rather, those who are curious will drive understanding and progress. They will be the natural leaders of our world, while the masses often remain content to follow like sheep.

The great differentiator between those who lead versus those who simply follow is often the thirst for information combined with the desire to learn. This is also the difference between those who experience the richness of life versus those who simply exist. Throughout history, we have witnessed the distinction between those who learn to get by and those who seize all that life has to offer. The descriptions may vary—from intellectual curiosity to lifelong learning to the Renaissance person—but the underlying principle is the same. Those who thirst for knowledge and fill their minds with a broad range of information have the power to change their own lives and the world in which they live.

CURIOSITY DRIVEN BY EMOTION

Ultimately, the behavior of curiosity is an emotionally driven action that can be traced to the origins of human development. The idea of curiosity-as-emotion is a mental and sometimes a physical experience that drives humans to seek out types of knowledge. This emotional quest for knowledge can be ongoing and self-fulfilling. In other words, as an individual expresses their curiosity and satisfies their desire for knowledge, they become emotionally driven to seek further knowledge. When emotion drives curiosity, it can have both positive and negative attributes. It is easy to understand the positive aspects of it. Imagine a person who loves classical music and wants to become an expert in the musical art form. She may even take it one step further and learn an instrument to supplement her classical music passion. This example shows how emotion can drive curiosity to reach a favorable result.

Yet this emotional drive is not for universal knowledge. Instead, individuals seek very specific knowledge that resonates with their individual life experience. In the hands of an autocrat or one seeking to control, this can have a dangerous or even a life-threatening outcome. Curiosity-as-emotion can also have a dark side, causing cult-like behavior. In this case, individuals may seek out only information or knowledge that fits their individual emotional need. This important concept identifies and may explain the cult-like following that leaders from Hitler to Castro to Hugo Chavez developed, much to the dismay of the outside world. Their followers were vulnerable to their emotional curiosity because they were inundated with lies and conspiracy theories. While they exercised intellectual curiosity, it was limited by the emotional drive to seek only that information that fit their emotional needs. This is a tribal behavior in which otherwise intelligent individuals will believe they are well informed, yet their curiosity is highly curated to seek only the answers that meet their pre-existing worldview.

As we have discussed throughout this book, fear is very real. It drives human behavior, both in the positive and negative sense. Unfortunately, fear can stifle our curiosity too. The antidote to this behavior is to make individuals aware of the phenomenon so that they can respond differently, learning to turn anxiety and fear into exploration and confidence. This is where the role of the individual becomes so important. We, as individuals, must be aware of this phenomenon, whether it is a dynamic in our friend group, our school, or our society. We must not give in to a belief that the system is rigged against us; rather, we should exercise our own self-determination to ignite our own intellectual curiosity to overcome whatever social barriers may exist, real or otherwise.

RECOGNIZE THE BARRIERS TO CURIOSITY AROUND US

Socioeconomic power, gender, class, race, or ethnicity can all stifle curiosity in one way or another. Throughout history, there have been governments and leaders known to suffocate individual curiosity to ensure that some groups don't get any "ideas" about who they are and what they might like to change about their positions in society. In classroom situations, the same dynamics can sometimes hold true based on ethnic, class or gender considerations.

Given these realities with the state of education, the role of the individual in taking charge of one's own destiny becomes even more critical. One could argue that curiosity may play an even greater role in individual self-determination if one must also overcome the bias or challenge of an institutional system that may be an obstacle in itself.

Think of curiosity as a caged animal, ready to spring free and play. Given this, it is crucial that we find our own mediums to allow curiosity to run wild. In doing so, we reduce the constraints that often eliminate curiosity from our lives. While curiosity alone is not sufficient to overcome all these obstacles, it will certainly provide the individual with a higher chance of achievement in classrooms and in the workplace. It will expand their minds to allow them more opportunities for creative thinking and to interact with the world in a much more engaged and healthy way. That is an important function, especially considering how quickly the world around us has expanded.

The contemporary world has frequently been described as "global," "connected," and even "flat" to represent the unique characteristics of our ability to travel both physically and virtually through space in ways that we had never conceived before.[14] In his book, *The World is Flat,* Thomas Friedman describes a world that has become "flat" as increased globalization has made it almost impossible to remain isolated from people who have different linguistic, cultural, or ethnic backgrounds.

Even if countries continue the current trend toward nationalism, the increasing power of technology brings other countries and cultures closer to us every day. SpaceX Starlink satellites are bringing internet connectivity to the farthest reaches of our globe. Meanwhile, cellular connectivity and signal strength will continue to improve, bringing us all closer together every day. This creative technology has produced the need for a new set of social skills that emphasize our ability to communicate across cultural divides, to be open to alternative points of view, and to show tolerance for those who are different from us; but we have a long way to go. This is curiosity on steroids. Through curiosity we can bring counties and cultures closer together toward one world view.

Is this even possible in an increasingly hostile world? Here is the solution: Let's celebrate the curious mind, the critical thinker, the individual steeped in self-determination who will not allow another person or people to determine his fate through lies and misinformation but instead seeks knowledge and truth. To instill a culture of

14 Thomas L. Friedman, *The World Is Flat: A Brief History of the Twenty-First Century* (Bridgewater, NJ: Distributed by Paw Prints/Baker & Taylor, 2009).

intellectual curiosity seeking knowledge and truth over misinformation and lies is indeed a self-help tool for humanity.

THE POWER OF WHY

Simon Sinek is an author and inspirational speaker who became famous for his book entitled *Start with Why*. In this book, he shows that leaders with the greatest influence across the globe share a common denominator. He describes a powerful idea that he calls the Golden Circle. This simple idea frames the three important questions that must be addressed in any endeavor...*why, how, and what*. In fact, the framework for *Education Is Freedom* is based on this same approach to encourage each of us to understand *why we learn, how to learn, and what to learn*. The idea of starting with *why* is grounded in the importance of curiosity. We must ask why. In turn, we must be able to explain why.

Simon Sinek describes *Start with Why* as being born out of pain. He had lost passion for his work and no longer found happiness in the occupation he had pursued for years. He explained that he had lost his "why" and began to let his curiosity pursue the reasons. Looking around, he realized that many of us were missing the why in our lives. He also recognized that leaders and organizations were muddling along in the absence of their own understanding of why. This was a spark that ignited his own curiosity and led him to teach the elements of curiosity to leaders around the world.

In the course of writing *Education Is Freedom*, I too had to begin with why. The very future of humanity depends on the continued growth of our individual and collective knowledge. With all of the confusion and debate about education today, the fundamentals of why, how, and what to learn have become obscured. I believed that it was timely and relevant to step back from the immediate challenges of society today and to explore the importance of education to our individual and collective freedom. I believe that each of us has unlimited potential that can be unlocked through knowledge. *THIS* is the *WHY* behind *Education Is Freedom*.

By the time we enter the workforce, our curiosity and therefore our creativity is sometimes muted and replaced with specialization or competence in a specific area of expertise. This specialization can be an obstacle to innovation and growth. In contrast, the evolution of most businesses is fueled by internal intellectual curiosity. Most of the discoveries and inventions throughout history, from invention of the wheel to the self-driving automobile, are the direct result of curiosity. The impulse to seek unique possibilities and to develop novel solutions is part of the human experience.

Francesca Gino, a behavioral scientist and professor at Harvard Business School, has highlighted research that points to three important insights about curiosity. First, she says, "Curiosity is much more important to an enterprise's performance than was previously thought." Second, by making small changes to the design of their organizations and the ways they manage their employees, leaders can encourage curiosity—and improve their companies. Third, although leaders may say that they treasure inquisitive minds, in fact most stifle curiosity, fearing it will increase risk and inefficiency.

In her *Harvard Business Review* article, Gino speaks to the importance for companies to foster a culture that encourages the question "why." The inspiration for the Polaroid instant camera, she said, was a three-year-old's question. Inventor Edwin Land's daughter wanted to immediately see a photo her father had just snapped. When he explained that the film had to be processed, she wondered aloud, "Why do we have to wait for the picture?"

Gino went on to describe a practice at Toyota called the "5 Whys" approach. Employees at the car company are asked to address problems by asking, "Why?" They must repeat that practice five more times until they thoroughly address the problem. This mindset fosters innovation through curiosity, challenging existing practices and procedures to foster continual improvement.

OUR RETURN TO CHILDHOOD

As children, we feel free to ask "why." Our curiosity is innate and fuels our ability to absorb critical information. We don't worry about what others think or whether we should already know the answer. Our insatiable thirst for knowledge constantly drives us to seek answers. Our families may tire of the constant "why, why, why" as we question everyone and everything around us. In fact, they may discourage all the questions and over time may inadvertently crush our inquisitive spirits. As we grow older and develop more self-confidence, often we become more and more reluctant to ask questions for fear of being judged for not already knowing the answers. Too often, by the time we are adults, our native curiosity is suppressed to our developmental detriment.

When it comes to curiosity, be a child. Reawakening the inner child's sense of wonder is essential for creativity to flourish. By embracing our innate curiosity, we open the door to endless possibilities. In doing so, you will uncover nuggets of unexplored information and new adventure. This sense of wonderment will be the impetus for your continued growth and evolution. So, always live a life with curiosity, expecting that every day may bring a new adventure.

CHAPTER 10

CREATIVITY: INTELLIGENCE AT PLAY

"Creativity is intelligence having fun."

Albert Einstein

If curiosity will cause us to ask *why*, then creativity will cause us to ask *why not*? No doubt, creativity is another of the most important human traits. Without the spark of creativity, there would be no innovation, no appreciation for beauty, no emotion in daily activities, and little if any progress. Without creativity, we would remain stagnant, unwilling or unable to discover anything new. It is our creative muscles that forge us ahead to new frontiers. Curiosity may have inspired early man to create the wheel, but creativity is the spark that that made it roll. If curiosity is what makes us wonder, then creativity is what helps us execute. Without the creative minds of our ancestors, we would still reside in the Stone Age, waiting for a creative mind to invent fire.

While at the heart of learning and education, we sometimes relegate the teaching of creativity as an unimportant elective. In fact, educators and educational programs sometimes discourage creativity in the interest of more technical training with real world applications. For many years we encouraged the importance of STEM education, focused on *Science, Technology, Engineering, and Math*. In recent years, many have modified the acronym to STEAM adding the

Arts as a nod to the importance of creativity in the learning process. How does one learn without finding creative solutions to complex problems? How does one stomach the tedium of rote memorization without finding creative ways to make it fun? Creativity is, indeed, intelligence having fun, with a huge emphasis on the word "fun."

Today I am an artist. I am not a professional by any means, but I enjoy the expression of creativity, the ability to let color and form take shape on a canvas. I still have a piece of my original art from childhood. I could not have been more than four or five years old when I attempted my first paint by numbers effort. The piece is a mess. Clearly, I had neither motor skills nor patience to stay within the lines of the paint-by-numbers instructions. But this small piece of art is beautiful to my adult eye. My mother or father would likely have been proud. Instead of chastising my poor art skills, they might have called me their future Impressionist. For whatever reason, I have no fear of creativity. It is ingrained in my existence, and I try to celebrate it each day. I am not sure how I eliminated the fear of being judged for creating, but that was my first major step in becoming an artist.

Once we overcome our fear of failure, we can explore and familiarize ourselves with a whole new world of creativity. Anyone can paint. Anyone can play a musical instrument or sing. Anyone can mold a block of clay into a form. We are all born as creative beings, but many of us are shamed out of such impulses as dancing or singing or painting at an early age. How often do we see a young person admonished for coloring outside of the lines? It happens frequently. How often does a parent hush their child when the little boy or girl is singing at the top of their lungs or dancing with reckless abandon? Are they encouraged to continue being creative, or are they told to be quiet? If children use crayons on the walls to create a masterpiece; do we respond by celebrating their creativity, or do we punish them for their actions? The answer is obvious—it is, at least in part, our fault as adults for extinguishing the growth and evolution of our younger generation's artistic spirit.

Long ago, science discovered that the human brain has two sides, a left and a right. Generally, one side of the brain controls the other side of one's body. Therefore, the left side of the brain controls the right hand. Most humans are right-handed, meaning the left side of their brain is the dominant part. The left side of the brain is thought to be more analytical, focused on logical thought, mathematics, and linear thinking. In contrast, the right side of the brain is more visual and intuitive. This is where the imagination holds court and is why the right side of the brain is thought of as the artistic or creative side.

We have diminished the importance of right brain activities such as art and music in our left-brain-oriented society. Often, the artist is thought of as unusual or odd, but the great irony is that both music and art have a fundamental basis in mathematics, requiring the artist to draw from both the left and right brain just to create. The technical aspect of art (the timing of a chord sequence or the geometry of artistic perspective) is a skill set that pulls from left brain technical skills. In contrast, the expressionism of music or the emotion an artistic masterpiece evokes are the result of right brain activity. Just as the left hander (driven by right brain activity) was thought of as odd and often encouraged to learn to use the other hand, the artist is often discouraged from practicing his art. Our society provides little positive reinforcement of right brain activity. We may try to dance and are laughed at when we fall flat on our face. We may try to sing and are told that we are off key. As a result, many of us build up a fear of failure and convince ourselves that we aren't good at artistic expression. As a result, we lose the right brain muscle memory as we go through life. Thankfully, this loss of creative impulse is not permanent. Once freed from the fear of failure, it simply becomes a matter of time invested and willingness to try. Meanwhile, in doing so, you exercise part of your brain that would otherwise lay dormant.

Today, perhaps more than ever, art plays an immeasurable role in our lives. From pure enjoyment of the arts to new product development, creativity is an amazing outlet for release and expression. If we are to fully learn about the world and our role in it, we must recognize and celebrate art. That begins with building our creative muscles and celebrating their remarkable benefits.

THE BENEFITS OF CREATIVITY ARE IMMEASURABLE

Whether we recognize it at first glance or not, creativity fosters many beneficial outcomes. From solving many of the world's most complicated problems, to innovation that drives new products and solutions, the more we bolster and expand our creative existence, the better for us all. A creative life is a more colorful life and a far more interesting life. To that end, I cannot overstate the true value of being creative, but here are some of its unequivocal highlights.

First, creativity can help build confidence. Art is an iterative process and the more we practice, the more we learn and the better we become. It is one of those skills where time and effort pay visual or aural dividends. In other words, you can see or hear your progress unlike the less tangible process of learning quadratic equations. Pretty soon we can sing or dance or paint so well that we can share that artistic expression with others. That process of sharing our expression becomes another form of communication.

As a sophomore in high school, I was teased into auditioning for a role in a play. By some miracle, I was selected to play the lead character named Joe Ferrone in *Up the Down Staircase*. Doing this on a lark, I became immersed in the fun of after-school rehearsals, never focusing on the reality of opening night when I would have to stand on that stage and bare my soul to a live audience. I was terrified when the reality set in. With the help of an excellent teacher/drama coach, I was also very well prepared, and the preparation took away my fear. Nothing builds one's confidence like the applause of an appreciative audience. I'm sure my performance was wildly amateurish, but the audience didn't care and applauded anyway. That applause stays with me today and makes public speaking a comfortable experience, a skill that I stumbled on by being teased into a random audition. Confidence building is a strong advantage of the arts, and it is a skill there for the taking.

Second, creativity can improve your overall state of well-being. Practicing art can stimulate your imagination and help you envision a more hopeful future. Creativity can help you navigate problems while aiding you in overcoming the fear that those problems trigger. There is no better therapy for stress than a few hours at the keyboard or behind an easel. Like meditation, practicing the arts can transport you emotionally to a different place by allowing you to focus on beauty and self-expression rather than to worry about worldly problems of the day.

Third, creativity can inspire us and those around us. The ability of artistic expression to touch our hearts is another way of opening doors. Through the visual arts or performing arts, you can appeal to others' emotions and reach them in ways that transcend the spoken word. Research has also linked creativity with the individual's motivation to learn. When students are working on a creative exercise, they become more focused and more driven to develop the skills they need to improve. They get immediate feedback on their progress and can more easily measure results.

Fourth, creativity can awaken and expand our senses. An artist can see light and shadows when others may see one dimension, have an awareness of colors that others can't detect, and possess an ability to hear things that others can't. The ability to exercise one's right brain makes a person more aware of the surrounding universe. Music goes from background noise to expression. Nature goes from simple weather patterns to the majesty of a breathtaking sunset. The arts will contribute to a higher state of being in all who participate, even in a modest way. Immersing yourself in art forms allows you to see different views of the world. Our senses are extremely powerful, and creativity further expands on them to give us even greater dimensional exposure.

Fifth, creativity balances us in an unbalanced world. Today, we have become specialists. At an early age, we are pushed to decide what we want to do. Too often, these decisions take us down a technical path that uses our left-brain capabilities but neglects the right. The result? An accountant, for example, who demonstrates excellent technical skills but struggles to understand how a budget could include a possible upside scenario. It isn't a coincidence that some of our most successful professionals have an artistic avocation as musicians, painters, or hobbyists. Their part-time use of their right brain keeps them balanced and gives them permission to be more creative in their otherwise technically driven decision-making processes.

Sixth, creativity is an essential job skill for the future. As technology and machines replace more and more manufacturing or physical labor roles, artificial intelligence will even threaten jobs in the technology sector. In any role, in any company, in any function, we need the creative thinker, idea generators and innovators, to help businesses progress. Technology can assist with information about customer preferences, but it is the creative mind that can put those preferences into ideas for new products or new ways to satisfy the customer.

CREATIVITY IN BUSINESS: THE WAVE OF THE FUTURE

In business, I have found that creativity provides individuals and companies with a competitive advantage. It is like having a camera with a superior lens that allows for a different focal point, letting you see things that may be invisible to others. It provides for more effective—if not balanced—decision-making because it allows all variables to be considered, both hard technical facts and softer nontechnical impressions.

Creativity can't be delegated to a department or individual within a company but instead must be part of a company's culture. A culture of innovation and responsiveness to change will allow a company to differentiate itself from competition and to successfully satisfy its stakeholders, both customers and shareholders. It is why some companies "wow" us with new ideas while others simply stay the same. Creativity serves several purposes, but primarily it is essential for innovation and growth. Innovation is almost impossible without some level of creativity involved in creating something new. Not all ideas are good ideas, but ideas are the fuel that will propel a company's success into the future.

At 7-Eleven, creativity was fundamental to our success. If you're in the convenience business, you must recognize that customers' need for convenience will change. Sometimes that change can be daily. If you want to see a creative response to change, walk the streets of New York City and watch the street vendors when a drop of rain begins to fall. Their sidewalk blanket filled with an assortment of trinkets and handbags suddenly disappears, replaced by an assortment of umbrellas. This is an example of pure retailing at its finest, with street vendors creatively responding to the changing needs of customers, in real time.

A corporation must be equally responsive. As customers' needs shift, a company must anticipate that and respond accordingly. At 7-Eleven, we created a culture of creativity, encouraging every employee and every franchisee to keep their antennae up, to always search for new products or new ways to satisfy the convenience needs of customers. When ATMs first became a new way to get cash, 7-Eleven was the first retailer to put a machine in every store, making it possible for customers to have ready access to cash. When we noticed customers pulling up in their Mercedes to buy beef jerky and pork rinds, we saw a trend toward low-carbohydrate diets. The company responded by collaborating with nutrition bar companies to create low-carb snack bars and began selling fresh, high-protein snack packs.

This creative process isn't limited to the marketing or merchandising team. Anyone can be creative. Once, while in Japan, I opened the hotel's small refrigerator late in the evening. My target in the darkened room was a simple bottle of water, but my hand pulled out a container that felt almost frozen to the touch. I turned on the lights and discovered a small aluminum container holding grapefruit juice. *Imagine,* I thought, *having a container like this for beer.*

I brought the container back to the US and shared it with representatives from Miller Beer and Anheuser-Busch. Both companies agreed that it was interesting, but neither moved forward quickly to help me test this unique packaging. Nearly two years passed, and I had still not found anyone to partner with 7-Eleven on the new packaging idea. This creative solution to selling cold beer was being caught up in our supplier's corporate inertia.

When August Busch IV scheduled a dinner, I saw the opportunity to make my pitch. At previous dinners with Anheuser-Bush senior executives, a silver champagne bucket was always present, filled with perfectly chilled longneck bottles. At this dinner, I brought in a second silver bucket filled with Budweiser beer, but it was all in the new aluminum bottles that we had packaged in Japan. A creative package was presented in a creative way. This captured the attention of the ultimate decision maker and resulted in the collaboration on a new package design that is now one of the most popular packages for beer. Since then, businesses from Coca-Cola to bottled water companies have adopted the package; all have tried to differentiate with a more creative solution for keeping beverages cold. Years later, when interviewed by the National Association of Convenience Stores, Busch said, "We found in research that this package was very appealing. It took beer into an image environment that traditional packages could not get into. I want to give credit to Jim Keyes with 7-Eleven, who brought the aluminum bottle idea to us."

Creativity in business is everyone's job. It isn't difficult or mysterious. In many cases, it is simply common sense and awareness of the opportunities before our eyes. If we ignite our own awareness of change, stimulate our own curiosity, have confidence to present the idea and present it with clarity, then each of us, at any level in the corporation, has an opportunity to help our company succeed.

CREATIVITY IS INSPIRING

Throughout history, creativity has been another form of communication and inspiration. Sacred art, for example, has been used for evangelization and to bring individuals' hearts and minds to faith. In ages past, moments from the life of Buddha, Muhammad, Moses, David, or Jesus have been depicted through art, architecture, music, and literature. In this form, creativity has been used to inspire, to inform, to evangelize, and to teach. Creativity has changed the world in ways often unimaginable. In recent years, I have had the privilege of working with the Vatican Art Museum in an effort to bring technology to the precious sacred art that one must otherwise travel to Rome to enjoy. One day soon, we hope to share the beauty of the Sistine Chapel or the Raphael Tapestries with the world outside of Rome through the use of immersive technology such as laser projection and virtual reality. Bishop Edward Burns of the Dallas Diocese described it best when he characterized this use of new technology to inspire and teach as the "modern-day stained-glass window." For thousands of years, the church has used stained glass as a tool for evangelization to inspire and teach. In the future, we will be able to accomplish the same through technology, sharing the beauty and teaching of art that was once available only to those able to visit museums.

The opportunity to nurture creativity surrounds us in everyday life. Art, music, literature, architecture, even the design or packaging of consumer products is an expression of creativity or a form of art that we encounter every day. One must simply open themselves up to the creative sources in our midst. Consider the many possibilities:

Museums are the amphitheaters of public education. Within the walls of a museum are the stories of history and the creative product of artists from around the world. Simply taking in the riches offered there can inspire and educate us.

Music is everywhere. The depth and range of musical alternatives, from classical to jazz to hip-hop, are all forms of expression that stimulate our hearts and minds. From the great concert halls of the world to earbuds on a flight, music can awaken our senses and open our hearts.

Architecture is a form of art often taken for granted because of its ubiquity. In Washington, DC, alone, we have a range of offerings, from the classic Roman influence of the US Capitol to the Egyptian-inspired Washington Monument to the modern National Museum of African American History and Culture.

Street Art is a form of expression too. What may appear to be graffiti is sometimes cherished by locals who see it as a creative expression. In fact, some of the most celebrated and special artists of the modern-day generation take great inspiration and style from these street artists who are creating on every corner in America.

Advertising is the creativity behind a television commercial, a billboard, or even a neon sign. Sometimes these forms of communication can become iconic, a part of the landscape. The CITGO sign just outside of Fenway Park is an unmistakable feature atop the left field wall known as the Green Monster. CITGO

Petroleum was a wholly owned subsidiary of the Southland Corporation, parent company for 7-Eleven. My career journey at 7-Eleven began shortly after the corporation acquired CITGO Petroleum as a source of gasoline for their stores. While in a strategic planning role for CITGO Petroleum, I learned that the company had decided to cut funding for the iconic sign and planned to tear it down. The city, when it heard this plan, was in an uproar. Boston natives had long identified the sign with Fenway Park and their beloved Red Sox. A Massachusetts native, I understood the passion but was still shocked at the city's willingness to keep the sign lit at taxpayer expense! CITGO decided to keep the iconic sign in place and everyone was happy. This is one of many examples that demonstrates the power of advertising as art.

Nature is possibly the most powerful expression of creativity. A breathtaking sunset, a rainbow appearing after the rain, and a beautiful white cumulus cloud on a summer day are all forms of nature's art. From the photography of Ansel Adams to the paintings of Georgia O' Keeffe, artists have captured the beauty of nature all over the world. The best part of nature, however, is the abundance of free art before our eyes every day. Next time you look at a bouquet of flowers, take a closer look into the symmetry of form and the explosion of color that exists within each individual bud or the intricate latticework that frames an individual leaf. As a pilot, I have my camera always handy in the cockpit. The images of nature from the air are awe inspiring and always evoke gratitude for the power of learning to give me the opportunity to see such beauty from the air.

Creativity is a form of expression, a way for people to connect to one another and the world around them. Dating back to the beginning of time, we used pictures on rock walls to communicate. Perhaps seen as one of the earliest art forms, these pictures not only told our story but did so through art. Some may even argue that art was the earliest method of communicating. We all understood pictures. And those same pictures they drew on rock walls centuries ago still make sense today. That shows the power of art. Go to any country in the world and, whether you can speak the native tongue or not, you can look at a piece of art and learn something about the culture, the people, or the message the artist tried to relay.

The idea is that creativity surrounds us and is there for the taking every single day, in everything we do and in everywhere that we go. All that we must do is open our eyes, open our hearts, and allow ourselves to be inspired and shaped by these omnipresent forces around us.

GETTING CREATIVE: A HOW-TO GUIDE

We are all born to be creative. Whether that skill remains dormant or is part of our everyday existence, we must acknowledge that we are creative. It is in the very fabric of our being. In some of us, the skill has simply remained inactive for years. Each of us can benefit from expanding our creative horizons.

The first step is to get out of your comfort zone. Pick a form of creativity that you think you're not good at, then do it. Don't think you can sing? Try karaoke. Don't think you can dance? Sign up for free dance classes. Don't think you can paint? Buy a canvas, paint, and brushes and pull up some old Bob Ross videos on YouTube. If you're of age, a glass of wine may accompany this exercise and help with a little liquid courage. As with most things in life, we grow and learn when we get out of our comfort zone. This is especially true in the arts. Try something new, even if it is scary or uncomfortable. The result will surprise you.

The second step is to practice. One advantage of practicing any form of artistic expression is that feedback is nearly instantaneous. When taking a sculpting class in Italy at the Florence Academy of

Art, I had spent days perfecting the nose and mouth on a bust I was creating out of clay. It didn't look so much like the model as it did a deformed humanoid, but I was proud of the work. I was crushed when my teacher came by to inspect it, then took a trowel and hacked off the entire face of my sculpture, telling me to start over. Painful as it was, he was right. My second effort was greatly improved, and the lesson stayed with me. Practice builds muscle memory and skill and ultimately builds confidence.

The third step is to make time for creativity. Exercise your creative instincts no matter where you are or what you're doing. This could be as simple as doodling while listening to a lecture or humming or singing while performing tasks like washing the dishes. There is always time for creativity if we make the time.

The last step is to always try something new. To be creative, we must move outside of our comfort zone. An unlimited array of art forms is waiting to be enjoyed. If you've mastered one form, try another. I will never be a professional-level musician, but I can pick up several instruments, from a guitar to a keyboard, and play with some modest degree of proficiency. Learning something new can be as enjoyable as perfecting something you know, and it can ignite a new level of interest and creativity as a result.

Creativity isn't a mysterious trait or something that is often passed on through genetics. We exist as creative beings, as individuals who want to learn, expand, grow, and explore. As we do so, we discover a world that is a wonderful and colorful version of our often black and white lives. It may seem unfamiliar at first, but it is some of the most fun you'll ever have. Creativity is truly, intelligence at play!

SECTION IV
WHY WE LEARN

Now that we have determined WHAT to Learn and HOW to Learn, we should return to the starting question of WHY We Learn. Knowing the WHY will inspire our ability to keep learning. The *what* and *how* of learning are internally focused, based on "self" and our ability to manage our internal motivations. The *why* causes us to turn outwards to consider the way we look at others and the way they perceive us. Few of us live in isolation, on the proverbial desert island without a need to interact with others. Instead, we live in a world of unique people, places, and cultures that can help us grow as individuals and allow us to succeed collectively as a society. The next three chapters focus on the world around us and how we, as individuals, can become better individually and, as a result, become better contributors to society.

- **Collaboration:** The idea that two minds are better than one holds true, but collaboration is often elusive for individuals because of the constant tension between individual interests and the good of the whole. The key to collaboration is the ability to share a common goal or objective. Collaboration and cooperation require putting one's individual interest second to the interests of the group.
- **Cultural Literacy:** The ability to understand, respect, and learn from other cultures will ultimately contribute to the cumulative learning that makes us "who" we are. We have a choice as individuals...to reflect the small group of individuals of our immediate circle (family, community, or even country) or to become a reflection of the cultural influences that contribute to the collective character of humanity. The more we learn of other cultures, the richer our own existence can be.
- **Character:** Integrity, the ability to develop intellectual honesty, is integral to the learning process. If we aren't

> honest with ourselves, we can't be honest with others. Honesty requires an open mind, a willingness to accept divergent points of view, and enough humility to know that we always have more to learn. Martin Luther King, Jr. encouraged us all to judge each other by our character, not by the color of our skin. Our character is ultimately the identity that we hold out for ourselves and for the world to see.

The question of *why* we learn is a multi-dimensional one. Of course, we learn to improve ourselves and our quality of life. That is the first dimension. The second dimension is that we learn to become better citizens. We learn to work through others and to recognize the value of community. We learn to appreciate other cultures and the collective strength of diversity. And finally, we learn the importance of character and the way the world sees us. That second dimension gives us the ability to navigate freely and comfortably outside of our personal orbit. The third dimension is the self-fulfilling prophecy of *why*. By seeking collaboration, cultural literacy, and character we come full circle to the original *why*. We are not in this world alone but share it with others and the more we learn from others, then the more we will learn for ourselves.

CHAPTER 11

COLLABORATION: BIGGER THAN THYSELF

"If you want to lift yourself up, lift up someone else."

Booker T. Washington

We have all heard the expressions, "Two minds are better than one," "One plus one equals three." Leadership expert and fellow Horatio Alger member, John C. Maxwell, introduced another way to express the act of working together toward a common goal. "Collaboration is multiplication," he says. The origin of the word *collaboration* comes from the Latin words *com* (with) + *laborare* (to labor, to work). Simply said, it is the process of two or more people, entities, or organizations working together to complete a task or achieve a goal. Often, this shared outcome is a superior effort, a product of multiplied energy. Collaboration, in its essence, is a team sport.

My first introduction to the power of collaboration came through the wonders of music. Beginning my musical journey at a very young age, I learned to play the flutophone, a small plastic flute that would make a miraculous sound to the ears of the player while squawking like a duck to any nearby listeners. My promise as an aspiring flutophone player quickly led to the opportunity to learn the trumpet, a beautiful brass thing of wonder. After pursing the lips and learning to breathe through the mouthpiece, I eventually produced a beautiful sound. The trumpet was an excellent vehicle to realize the fundamentals of music as I practiced scales and tried to choke out the occasional Beatles song. But, as I would soon recognize, "Hey Jude" just doesn't sound the same on a solo trumpet.

Eventually, I progressed enough to join the grammar school band in Grafton, Massachusetts. Not exactly the Boston Symphony Orchestra, but our little group produced the magic of orchestral music. With other students, I quickly discovered the power of collaboration. Alone, my solo trumpet was brassy and loud, but the unison of our orchestra produced a harmony that made us all sound like musicians! It was a miracle. It was a lesson. Two instruments are better than one. Twenty instruments are better than two.

Multiple instruments can play different notes in harmony, creating a richer and fuller sound than any one instrument. The combined sound of the many talented musicians playing together can mask the flaws of one instrument that may be out of tune. In summary, the orchestra taught me that the whole is greater than the sum of its parts. Now, you don't have to play an instrument to understand what I am describing.

I was fortunate to progress over the years from the flutophone, to the trumpet, to keyboards, and eventually have the privilege of serving as Chairman of the Dallas Symphony Orchestra. My introduction to the Dallas Symphony came through a new program they were launching called Young Strings. They were raising money to provide instruments to underprivileged students in the public school system, with members of the orchestra volunteering their time to provide instruction. This collaborative effort to bring music education to those who couldn't afford the privilege spoke volumes to me. The trumpet made available to me in my grammar school in Grafton, Massachusetts was a gift, paid for by a member of the Boston Symphony. The generous musician, Mr. Fred Orkiseski, who was also a part-time music teacher in this small rural school, would occasionally provide help for needy students who could not otherwise afford music training or their own instruments. It was many years later that I became aware of this one musician's generosity that gave me the opportunity to learn, so of course, I readily agreed to support this program in Dallas. It was an example of opportunity coming full circle and a chance to pay it forward for others. The Young Strings program brought me awareness of the positive influence of collaboration in my life and in the future of these young students.

Sitting in the acoustical sweet spot of the I.M. Pei–designed Meyerson Concert Hall, one of the finest music halls in the world, I could witness this power of collaboration come to life. A single Young Strings violinist broke the silence, then a second and third violin joined in, soon to be accompanied by a group of cellos, and then a bass. The sound of strings became more complex, and the richness of multiple instrumental voices filled the ears. Then the brass section came to life along with percussion, and the lilting sound of an oboe rose above the blend. The result is an orchestral harmony sound that could not be created by one instrument or any single musician.

Collaboration is indeed multiplication; it is the power of many acting as one. This same power of collaboration causes businesses to excel, artists to create, scientists to discover, and sports teams to win championships. It has been said that star athletes can win games but only teamwork can win championships. Technology today makes it even more possible to collaborate, even when groups (or teams) are separated by time and distance.

THE TOOLS OF COLLABORATION

Technology has made it possible to achieve this multiplier effect in ways never imagined in the past. In fact, the internet itself was a product of collaboration. It serves as both an example of the power of collaboration and valuable tool to help facilitate collaboration. Before the internet, access to information through technology was limited by proprietary silos. You were either working in DOS or creating your own discovery tools by coding in COBOL or Fortran. The idea of open systems and shared access was once taboo and thought of as heresy.

Scott McNealy, cofounder of Sun Microsystems, was an early advocate of the idea to create a networked environment. At Sun, he focused on the network rather than the computer, meaning that open systems and the power of collaboration would exponentially increase the productivity and power of computing. Sun was a proponent of open systems and open-source software that made the internet the ultimate form of an open-system network. Scott was ahead of his time and recognized the power of collaboration in technology to advance both systems and opportunity. Today, Scott has turned his attention to using collaborative technology in the same way to transform education. He founded Curriki, an online, open education service that encourages collaboration among content providers and developers to provide transformative content, free to students all over the world.

With the development of social media platforms, the internet has become a forum for collaboration and social interaction. It has also provided a tool for collaborative projects, from marketing efforts to participative gaming to a broad range of group problem-solving. Collaboration has never been easier, but for some it remains an elusive art. It has never been as important to us individually and collectively. Here are some examples of the benefits of working together:

> *Problem-solving*: Whether trying to understand the solution to a quadratic equation or working on the turnaround of a multibillion-dollar corporation, collaboration is an essential ingredient to success. You will find that whenever a group of individuals works together to leverage their knowledge, ability, or ideas, then solutions that were previously unseen may come to light.

Learning: Diversity of thought creates learning. We often learn more from our peers than from our teachers. We each have something special to contribute, even if it does not appear on the surface. Teamwork, as a result, becomes a learning experience.

Efficiency: It may take an individual twice as long to solve a problem that a collaborative group could solve in half the time. Division of tasks can make us more productive, allowing the team to accomplish more, faster and better than the individual.

Innovation: Ideas are seldom created from within. The best ideas are often inspired by external people, places, or things that stimulate a spark. Even when triggered from within, the spark will turn into the flame of an idea faster and more effectively with the collaboration of others.

Acceptance/Buy-in: Humans have a natural resistance to change. Often, an individual's best ideas are crushed by the negative perceptions of a group dismissing an idea if not socialized effectively by the larger body. When a team proffers an idea, there is a greater chance of credibility and ultimate acceptance. At a minimum, there is a streamlined process of buy-in because a consensus has already been established through collaborative effort.

Morale/Attitude: Humans are, by nature, generally happier to work in groups. As a result, solving problems together will foster an improvement in morale and a higher level of satisfaction within individuals who can now take personal credit for the success of the team.

Checking even one of these boxes would prove to enhance productivity and increase the chances you'll eventually reach your goals.

In today's technology-driven world, collaboration is easier and also more important than ever before.

COLLABORATION BUILDS CULTURE/IDENTITY

Whether we are referencing the workplace, home life, or anywhere else, collaboration builds culture. We see this cultural influence most visibly in our allegiance to a favorite sports team, to our alma mater, to our place of employment, or to our national identity. Among any of these examples, we often take on the identity of the group and wear it proudly. This may be a physical symbol such as wearing our team's logo on game day or flying the flag outside of our home.

This collective culture does not just happen. Rather, a concerted effort builds through the individuals within the group who take on a collective identity. This happens through the decision to create an environment that gives team members the opportunity to communicate openly and honestly. If they form meaningful bonds with each other and with the group, they are more likely to take positive actions that benefit the whole.

A culture of high performance is the result of team members feeling safe to share their ideas to the point that no idea is bad. There is also an acceptance of mistakes as a learning opportunity that helps the team correct those mistakes together and perform more effectively going forward.

A successful collaborative culture is built by the tone at the top, as leadership sets the tone by example. In highly collaborative organizations, leaders deploy tools to help team members at all organizational levels, resulting in a culture that champions collaboration by leveraging each team member's unique skills. A successful team culture enjoys the multiplicative power of working collectively to produce the highest result possible.

If, in contrast, there is more truth in the hallways or locker rooms than in team meetings, leadership has not been successful in creating a culture of collaboration. Finding ways to have everyone embrace open and honest communication is essential. Building a culture of success requires several key elements:

Engagement is essential. Team members must be in or out. Even those on the sidelines for any given play must be engaged, at least mentally if not physically. The team must be fully vested in collective success.

Communication—from the top, from the bottom, and from peer to peer—is fundamental to the collective success of the team. Team members must feel comfortable communicating openly. They must feel safe expressing their ideas and trusting each other to fulfill their respective roles.

Information sharing and the proactive dissemination of knowledge among the team will contribute to the culture of mutual benefit. This environment will reward competency and the open sharing of best practices.

These behaviors result in a culture that those on the outside can see and feel. They will notice a group, a company, a team, or even a classroom as a dynamic unit that can accomplish any task. The culture of collaboration will create a culture of success. This virtuous cycle builds and builds, making both the individuals and the group continue to grow and succeed. For a group and then individuals within to succeed, everyone must share the common attitude "don't quit." We are in this together, and we will prevail must be the winning attitude of the day.

COLLABORATIVE CONFLICT

At times, collaboration can create conflict rather than resolution. When "don't quit" becomes the mantra for "we are right and they are wrong," then we may encounter stalemate versus progress. Unlike our support for sports teams or gaming, most of life's opportunities for collaboration are not binary right/wrong or win/lose propositions. In contrast, the progress of humanity into the future often requires collaboration outside of our immediate circle of influence. This is when the degree of difficulty increases and when all elements of the C-Suite Learnings come into play including our ability to embrace *change*; *confidence* to prevail over fear; *clarity* to help communications; *critical thinking* to separate fact from fiction; and for *curiosity* and *creativity* to stimulate the drive for *collaborative* solutions.

When it comes to education, the success of the student, the teachers, the school, and even the community calls for collaboration. A common purpose guides them. All members of the academic community, from teachers to administrators to students and to the community at large, should share a common vision for what the education experience should accomplish. In a healthy educational culture, they will work together toward a strategy with measurable goals that contribute to students' individual and collective successes. They will foster a culture of open dialogue in which the most critical educational matters are openly and honestly discussed. Individuals, from school board members to administrators to parents, will approach these discussions with mutual respect and trust. When there is disagreement, stakeholders still listen to one another because they believe deeply that respect for differences is part of the success criteria for moving their school forward. This culture of educational collaboration may seem like a dream in today's world of divisive politicization of our education system.

In contrast, we sometimes see groups band together into what I've described as collaborative conflict. Rather than having mutual respect for our differences, we witness fights over issues like critical race theory, parental rights, and affirmative action. These culture war issues can turn our schools into a battleground where parents, teachers, and school board members bring conflict rather than collaboration to the forefront. This is not to minimize these issues or indicate they are not important, but conflict can create its own culture—a culture of division, anger, and controversy that does little to advance the collective education of our children. Certainly, we all agree that the issues are important to surface and that problems are important to solve; however, we should take a page from an earlier chapter and acknowledge that it is not change that matters but how we respond to change that makes the difference between success and failure. In the same fashion, many of the changes we see in our schools do not matter as much as how we respond to the changes. Our mutual objective should be to create an environment that fosters improvement in learning across the board.

Still, sometimes we are not as fortunate to be involved in a culture of collaboration. Just as some of us are born into wealth while others are born into poverty, some of us will have the benefit of education in a culture of collaborative success and others will find themselves in a dysfunctional academic environment where politics prevails over academic preparation. In the latter environment, we must still take individual responsibility to create our own success culture. Each of us has the opportunity and the ability to create our own culture and our own identity. When you find yourself in a culture of failure, create your own identity and build your personal culture of success. We can share our identity with the group, but that shared culture must never take the place of our own individual identities.

You have a choice when the culture of your school, your work, or your team begins to crack. The first impulse might be to become a victim of your environment and adopt that adverse culture as your own. You may also be lured into taking sides. There is no win or lose in these culture battles. The dark side of collaboration is when it results in "sides" that end up pitting one team against another. Instead, you can take a leadership role within the group and foster a collaborative approach for the whole to create a new cultural identity for the group. The key is to rise above the group's cultural shortcomings to create your own success. That success will still rely on collaboration, but it will be up to you to foster that collaboration among your peers to do the best you can, given the challenging environment. Leadership is about uniting rather than dividing.

FAILURE TO COLLABORATE

So, this begets the question: Why don't we collaborate all the time? If collaboration is so powerful and can change so much, why is it such an elusive behavior? For several reasons we choose (or don't choose) to collaborate. And let me be clear, collaboration is a choice.

Ego, jealousy, greed, and fear are all enemies of collaboration. These emotional responses will erode the effectiveness of a team and detract from the success of the whole. We will never overcome the power of human emotion, but we can identify the behaviors that serve as obstacles to our success.

Ego may be the most pervasive of the many reasons we do not collaborate. Collaboration usually fails when one or more members of a group let their ego get in the way of trying new things or being open to new ideas. If we compare our abilities to others in the group, we may decide that we have more to give than to receive. Our own ego may cause us to dismiss the value or contribution of our peers. If so, we miss the opportunity to ignite our own imagination.

Jealousy is simply another form of self-interest. If we are afraid that another in the group will get more attention, more praise, or more success, then we are naturally inclined to pull back and protect our own self-interest. Collaboration then fails because individuals are more focused on their vested interests rather than focusing on the greater good.

Greed is a more dangerous form of self-interest. We compromise the outcome when individuals focus exclusively on their own benefit over that of the team. When that inside voice is popping up to ask, "Are you sure you are getting as much as the other person?" ignore it and work toward a collaborative outcome. The result will always help us accomplish more than we individually thought possible.

The worst of the obstacles that often comes across as greed or self-interest is, instead, fear. Our fear of differences between each other. Our fear of failure. Our fear of exposing our own weaknesses to the group. Our fear of others' motivations. They cause a fundamental lack of trust and a resulting lack of alignment, which further erodes collaboration.

> When your integrity and values are
> not aligned...
>
> When you have different goals or ideas...
>
> When you are driven by ego, jealousy, greed,
> or fear...

Then collaboration will fail, and you will revert to individual thinking or subgroup collaboration, which often leads to suboptimal outcomes. Collaboration requires transparency and a fundamental desire to work with others inside and sometimes outside of your immediate circle. One of those transparencies must be a clear understanding of why you should collaborate, and then an understanding of how and what to collaborate on. If collaboration partners are clear on the "why," then the "what and how" will naturally take care of itself.

I have done my best to recognize the value of collaboration throughout my academic and professional career, with a long list of successes and a few failures to share. Even in business we must sometimes look for opportunities outside of the boundaries of our own corporation. One example that comes to mind is the missed opportunity for collaboration between Netflix and Blockbuster. There have been many stories written about Netflix approaching Blockbuster with an offer to sell or merge their business. My predecessor, the former CEO at Blockbuster declined the opportunity at the time and history has not been kind to the assessment of that decision. During that time, Netflix was still selling subscriptions for DVDs to be delivered by mail. Blockbuster had the same capability and technically didn't need Netflix technology to provide the same offering. Hindsight is always twenty-twenty, but I can't fault that CEO's decision made with the information he had at the time.

When I arrived at Blockbuster, I reached out to the Netflix CEO, Reed Hastings, and re-initiated those discussions. The differences in the companies' two models could have made for an ideal collaboration. Netflix could have provided the older long-tail movies at a subscription price and Blockbuster could have provided the new releases at a pay-per-view or on-demand price. The result of that combination would have been a one-stop-shop for digital streaming, an offer that doesn't exist today. In other words, one online offering under the Netflix/Blockbuster brand could have provided a much broader range of old movies, new movies, television, and original content, and like the legacy Blockbuster store, a one stop shop for easy access to your favorite media content. By then, however, Netflix equity value had far surpassed the valuation of Blockbuster, making a combination much more difficult for either company to accomplish. While collaboration with Netflix was not in the cards, we went on to explore many other collaboration opportunities recognizing that partnership would have provided a faster path to success.

While a Blockbuster/Netflix combination wouldn't have been credited with saving humanity or bringing peace to the planet, there are many other examples of collaboration that could accomplish exactly that!

NOW BACK TO EDUCATION: TIME TO COLLABORATE

When it comes to academics, most of us see education as an individual activity. We take part in classes but are generally graded on individual performance. In business school the use of case studies is an effective tool to encourage and teach collaboration. Subgroups of students, often from diverse backgrounds, are asked to come together to solve a business problem outlined in a case study. At Columbia Business School, where they also use the case study approach, I remember a case that called for the analysis of two companies in the same industry but with two vastly different balance sheets. I was not accustomed to solving problems in a team setting and did not know how or where to begin. We had a professional accountant in our group, so I felt confident in his technical skills. In stark contrast, I remember feeling intimidated because I had not taken a single accounting class in college.

Ultimately, reaching the finish line required technical knowledge. Had it not been for our CPA-trained group member, we would have been in trouble. In addition to this technical training, however, the solution required an element of creativity. Working late into the night, I stumbled upon a creative way to factor the balance sheets, putting them both on par so that we could make a simple line-by-line comparison. Our team scored an A on the project, but the greatest reward was seeing how our collective teamwork created a higher level of performance and a greater chance for success.

Professor Peter Drucker was one of the most famous business academics. A lifelong student of business, *BusinessWeek* magazine described him as "the man who invented management." I had the privilege of visiting Professor Drucker at his home, just weeks before he passed away in 2005.

Always curious, he wanted to learn about 7-Eleven and the elements of our success. As we discussed the company's achievements, he was complimentary about my use of "we" when describing the collective success of my team. "Leaders who work most effectively," he reflected, "never say 'I.' And that's not because they have trained themselves not to say 'I.' They do not think 'I.' They think 'we'; they think 'team.' They understand their job to be to make the team function. They accept responsibility and do not sidestep it, but 'we' gets the credit. This is what creates trust, what enables you to get the task done." It requires self-confidence to accomplish this, the belief that you do not need to seek credit for any success. Rather, your recognition will come from the success of the team.

CREATING A BETTER SOCIETY

Through collaboration, we can begin to address and even solve some of the most difficult challenges facing humanity. Throughout history, miraculous things happen when government, business, and science come together to carry out a common goal. Notable examples of scientific collaboration include the International Space Station (ISS), ITER (an international nuclear fusion research and engineering mega project), and the European Union's Human Brain Project. One collaborative project that was believed to have the potential to bring peace to the world was the Manhattan Project. The harnessing of atomic energy to create weapons capable of mutual mass destruction was believed to be the answer to world peace. Instead of global collaboration to prevent mutual destruction, we ended up with a Cold War and a standoff that continues today. Sadly, a global collaboration of scientists could have continued to advance the positive science of nuclear energy during the past fifty years. Had we taken that approach, then perhaps we would have advanced our understanding of nuclear energy and fusion to be able to power the world rather than destroy it.

In recent years, technology has brought us a new opportunity for collaboration *or* for mutual destruction: *artificial intelligence*. Recently, a group of industry leaders from OpenAI, Google, and other artificial intelligence labs testified before Congress about the "risk of extinction" posed by this powerful new technology. They warned that future systems could be as deadly as pandemics or nuclear weaponry. They are calling for governmental oversight and regulation before the technology spins out of control to destroy humanity. The problem is that any one country seeking to regulate may find itself vulnerable to the whims of any other country that chooses to go rogue. This conundrum speaks to the critical nature of global collaboration. Only if we work together as one human race to address the power of this new technology will we stand a chance of managing its use into the future.

Here is the irony. The power of artificial intelligence has the ability to change the world in so many positive ways. It can help scientists develop new medicines to wipe out disease. It can accelerate development of fusion technologies to provide safe, low cost, carbon free energy. Most exciting given the focus of this book is the potential for artificial intelligence and machine learning to transform the way we teach and learn. The power of good behind this new technology is just as real as the power of evil. There is only one way to manage this balance of good and evil—through collaboration.

If the advent of artificial intelligence causes nations to come together in collaboration to avoid mutual mass destruction, then the outcome *could* be the ultimate benefit to humanity—world peace. Could humanity learn from our past experience after development of the atomic bomb? Could artificial intelligence and the real risk of mutual mass destruction this time force a collaboration among the nations of the world to work toward practical governance solutions? Or, in contrast, will AI become the next weapon of mass destruction that some nations use as a deterrent and others use as a threat? One thing is certain: world peace will never exist without collaboration. With collaboration, we shine a light in the darkness to end fear, foster trust, and empower the multiplier effect of great minds working together. The greatest beneficiary for the future of humanity is "us."

While the prospects of global collaboration and world peace are wonderful thoughts, you might ask how this concept relates to you. So, how does one individually work toward accomplishing this multiplier effect? As with most steps toward a better "me" or a better "we," our success or failure will rest with the execution. In other words, what we do rather than what we say is what counts. Here are three steps you can take toward improved collaboration.

The *first step* is awareness of the opportunity, a fundamental belief in the power of many coming together as one. The *second step* is the ability to put our fear and our egos aside to recognize that we have much to learn from others. The *third step* is to establish trust. We must trust others on the team, and, in turn, we must move forward with the integrity and transparency that will inspire others to trust us. Only then can we enjoy the multiplier effect of collaboration. Only then will we enjoy the full benefit of our own success and the success of those around us. Only then will we be a society of collaborators that places the collective good of us all above the need for individual gain or recognition. This, and world peace, requires a keen sense of appreciation for the differences that others bring to the table.

CHAPTER 12

CULTURAL LITERACY: WEAVING YOUR QUILT OF DIVERSITY

"We have become not a melting pot but a beautiful mosaic. Different people, different beliefs, different yearnings, different hopes, different dreams."

Jimmy Carter

Much of the learning journey outlined to this point has called for us to look inward. Even if we commit to learn from others, we may still fall short of truly understanding different people. We live in a patchwork quilt of diversity, which requires us to have an understanding of others I call cultural literacy. This literacy is about understanding the differences that make us one human race. To work together as one people on this planet, we must prevent the spread of ethnocentrism, the belief that one culture is superior to another. Our truth, then, should be a love for what is familiar but a relentless desire to learn more about other people, cultures, and practices.

Each of us, as individuals, embodies the genetic makeup of our physical being through our DNA. Each of us also, as individuals, embodies the intellectual makeup of the people around us. Both our physical and intellectual composition are likely to represent a woven patchwork of physical and intellectual influence that make us who we are. Before the advent of DNA markers, we all grew up believing that our race or our culture was directly related to the ethnicity of our parents. In recent years, tools like Ancestry.com and 23andMe have made it possible to scientifically explore our ancestral journey. Most of us will be shocked by the breadth of diversity in our genetic makeup. Few of us are genetically "pure."

Many are surprised to learn that they have a percentage of Ashkenazi Jewish ancestry, for example, even if they have no known Jewish heritage. Others, like me, learn that their heritage includes African, Middle Eastern, and even some Asian origins, likely tracing back generations. As more of us become aware of our actual ancestry, perhaps we will realize that we are all fortunate to have multicultural genetic origins that make us more unique and yet bring us together as one. In the words of Rosa Parks, "I believe there is only one race—the human race."

Even more important is our intellectual makeup. You've often heard that we are what we eat. Certainly, that can be true. However, a more relevant and appropriate statement would be that we are what we experience. Those with whom we interact become a part of us. We are the cumulative being of those who have influenced us in both good and bad ways. The more diversity of thought and culture we experience, the more complex and colorful the intellectual quilt that we weave. Diversity in our lives, if we embrace it, contributes to our individual cultural literacy. That cultural literacy, the ability to move freely from region to region and interact freely with people from all over this planet, is what exponentially increases our freedom as people of this one world.

Once we understand the power of cultural literacy, we can embrace the strength of our own capabilities while also being respectful of others' contributions. Other people, other races, other religions, and other cultures can all contribute to our individual and collective success. We are all part of one type of classification:

humanity. If we choose to share in our collective responsibilities as humans, we become empowered to create the greatest version of our lives and our world.

When traveling for business to Japan for many years, I was often surprised by the cultural differences seen in the boardroom. There was often misunderstanding and sometimes distrust between the American management team and their Japanese counterparts. Learning the Japanese language helped to open my eyes to much of this cultural difference. Becoming immersed in the Japanese culture whenever possible also helped me understand that our "differences" weren't really differences as much as they were points of uniqueness. I learned that translation in many of the Asian languages is not direct translation as we enjoy in Latin-based languages like Spanish or French. Instead, translation from Japanese to English is more "interpretation" because there are few direct word comparisons to the English language. The result can mean confusion or misunderstanding if one doesn't try to understand the intent as well as the words of an interpreter. The simple act of becoming aware of those unique cultural nuances helped immensely.

After many years of doing business across the globe, I became accustomed to using a different style of communication when in other countries. My tone is less forceful when speaking. I speak English slowly and articulate words clearly to facilitate translation. I strive for an air of humility in my approach. This is simply a sign of respect for my foreign hosts. I wasn't told to do these things. They came naturally as I traveled to other countries and observed their unique cultural practices. I was inherently curious about the culture and customs of each country I worked with. In turn, I made an effort to adapt in a way that would garner greater acceptance of my message.

In contrast, while traveling in other countries we have all witnessed our peers fall short of this cultural sensitivity. It is painfully awkward to witness a fellow American lash out at a waiter for not being able to speak English, even though we are guests in a foreign country. This is not a failure of intelligence, for many of these travelers are highly intelligent individuals with advanced degrees from prestigious universities. We can't really assign blame for their cultural ignorance but instead should encourage them to develop cultural literacy. Understanding and sensitivity are skills that can be learned, but awareness is certainly a prerequisite.

DEFINING OUR CULTURE

Culture is an essential part of what makes us who we are as individuals, families, countries—and as earthlings. Sometimes we define it by geography, like your nation, your state, your city, or even your neighborhood. Someone from New York City can be from the Bronx or from Brooklyn, and their culture can be completely different even though we're talking about two areas that are separated by mere miles.

Sometimes we define our culture by association. It could be a friend group, a motorcycle gang, a tribe, or perhaps a sport team. We feel an identity with the culture of that group. We can base culture on race as well, like understanding the distinct cultures that make up the African-American, the Latino, the Asian-American, the Italian-American, or other communities. None of these individual cultures are homogenous. For convenience or perhaps for census reasons we sometimes try to "categorize" entire cultures. Those of Latino heritage are sometimes called "Hispanic." I once made the mistake of referring to a friend with Cuban origins as Hispanic, but was quickly chastised. She reminded me that the Cuban culture and people were unique. Their culture and customs were very different from those of Puerto Rico, Mexico, or Spain. She was Cuban and proud of her heritage. Regardless of the name, all these various cultures become part of the fabric of the American dream. America is a place where most of us are here through immigration, even if it goes back generations. Together, each of us contributes to a collective culture. Forget the melting pot analogy. Think of it more as an American quilt, with everyone's culture stitched together to cover us all. But what happens when certain groups think that only their culture should be the predominant fabric of that American quilt and then become fearful of another's cultural influence?

Let's go back to September 11, 2001. Four coordinated attacks by the terror group al-Qaeda, led by Osama bin Laden, killed nearly three thousand people when four hijacked airliners crashed into the New York Twin Towers; the Pentagon in Washington, DC; and a Pennsylvania field. These nineteen hijackers, from Saudi Arabia, Egypt, Lebanon, and the United Arab Emirates, changed the psyche of this country forever. It's hard to measure the impact the terror attacks of 9/11 had on this country. The 9/11 survivors, those who experienced the suffering firsthand, will eventually pass on and memories will fade with them. Children born after 9/11 already look at it as a historical footnote, and the resonance continues to lessen. Today, many of us view 9/11 more as a past event than a traumatic experience.

So, what did this traumatic event have to do with culture or cultural diversity? Plenty, as I'd soon find out. As CEO of 7-Eleven at the time, I'd heard all the jokes about who and what we were. So, I'd developed a thick skin for the jokes, except for one that cut to the bone.

I was on stage to receive the Obelisk Award for my work in the arts. None other than Jay Leno presented me with the prize before a packed audience at the Meyerson Symphony Center in Dallas. I had to walk backstage, award in hand, to return to my seat, and by the time I arrived, uproarious laughter filled the air. "What happened?" I asked my wife as I took my seat next to her. "Leno just told a joke saying, 'Can you believe it? A 7-Eleven person who can speak English!'" He told the joke while I was walking backstage, so I hadn't heard him.

Leno wasn't the first or the last comedian to make fun of the fact that the 7-Eleven company had a lot of first-generation franchisees, many from the Middle East. From *Saturday Night Live* skits to your run of the mill stand-up comedian doing her five minutes at your local comedy club, foreigners at 7-Eleven were often the punchline. It was a joke that no one pushed back on, including 7-Eleven. Some may have held a belief that first-generation immigrants weren't really part of the fabric of this American quilt, so why not laugh at their expense? Who did it really hurt? How mistaken we all were.

First, it started with bricks. Our corporate headquarters' phones were inundated with reports that Americans were throwing bricks through 7-Eleven storefront windows right after 9/11, and for the life of us, we could not understand why. Mobs, angry at the terrorists, decided to take out their fears by targeting 7-Elevens. Why? Soon we realized that the target was people of Middle East origin who owned many of our franchises—hard working, innocent people who had nothing to do with the terrorist attacks. One of the most disturbing of incidents happened in Philadelphia, when an off-duty cop held a gun to the head of a Sikh franchise owner, telling him to go back to his own country. The gentle man, a peace-loving franchisee from India, couldn't be further removed from the terrorists who flew into the Twin Towers.

It was a catastrophe; a catastrophe not of our own making, but of an ignorance within our own country about how important our collective culture is to who we are. In the same way that people laughed at the idea that immigrants were part of the 7-Eleven culture, these people throwing bricks and holding guns were saying they were a direct threat. Those jokes, those descriptions, that mocking had boomeranged back on us and our employees. Except the real threat, when it comes to America, is cultural ignorance—a cultural ignorance that can turn violent when given a chance.

From as early as preschool to when you're in graduate school, you spend years in a classroom filled with children, young adults, and then full-fledged adults. Most of us fail to realize that our classmates are walking gold mines, holding one of our country's most valuable assets: our distinct and undeniable differences. If only we were to look at our differences as treasures, we would find that those differences are a treasure we can share.

CULTURAL CURRENCY: MORE IMPORTANT THAN WEALTH

To build our cultural literacy, we must have an openness to learning about the unique culture of others that share our community, our nation, or our planet. As we learn about others, we build a currency of knowledge about their uniqueness. To me, cultural currency is just a fancy term for accepting the unique offerings of all human beings, and more importantly, discovering how they can add value to who you are as a person. You come into this world a tabula rasa, or blank slate, and you yearn to be filled with positive cultural influences that expand your critical thinking, your ability to relate to others, your decision-making, and your ideas about what can make you and your community happy. If you surround yourself with only those who look, act, and think like you then you will become a reflection of that narrow subset. If, instead, you seek to surround yourself with those of other cultures and backgrounds then you too will develop a breadth of experience that reflects the cumulative strengths of each. All of that represents the cultural currency that can grow over time as you gain exposure to new and different cultures.

If you become aware of the unique offerings of every individual, you can take a little of each of them with you to weave your own individual cultural quilt. You and your identity can reflect the best that each individual and the world has to offer. For me, there are three key steps to achieving cultural currency:

1. *The Spark*: This is the initial big bang that puts cultural currency on your radar, but unfortunately, most people

aren't attuned to paying attention to it. It requires you to be "present" with your observational senses. What does it mean to be present? It means always being aware and engaged. The spark is that something that hits you when you are open to the experience. Perhaps a classmate, with a family heritage from the Philippines, brings lumpia spring roll for lunch and invites you to have a taste. Those who are closed to the spark reject the invitation without a second thought. Your job is to build your own cultural identity by being open to the bite. Savor the textures, the flavors, the smells, and then move to the next step.

2. *Reflection*: It's not enough to appreciate the taste of the lumpia spring roll. It's important to think about it. Think about the ingredients. Think about the people who made it. Think about why you believe it's an important dish for someone tied to the Philippines. Reflection adds experience to your personal cultural DNA. That lumpia doesn't make you Filipino or of Filipino heritage, but it connects you to people who are. Your reflections on this single bite then allow you to see your fellow classmate in a broader context. You've bitten into a tiny part of something that is important to her cultural life. What other doors are to be opened just from this one person and their experience?

3. *The Deep Dive*: This requires that you open cultural doors about the Philippines that go far beyond the spring roll that was the spark. Ask yourself, what can you learn about their lives, their struggles, their sense of community? Where is the Philippines located? What's their language, their religion, their global perspective? What does it mean to be a Filipino American?

Our cultural differences should not separate us but instead should bring us a collective strength for the good of all of humanity.

This cultural literacy is not automatic. It requires being exposed, understanding, and then developing interest and empathy toward people who may have different cultural experiences. Culturally deficient people, like the ones who threw bricks through the 7-Eleven windows or the man who couldn't distinguish a Sikh from a Saudi (even though India and Saudi Arabia are about two thousand miles apart), lack the humanity that comes from a lifetime of gained cultural currency.

Cultural ignorance is real. It surrounds us every day. It has always been a reality of humankind to be initially ignorant beyond the things most immediate to us. But that doesn't mean that we must remain culturally ignorant. Let's go back to that situation at 7-Eleven. In my case, the spark shouldn't have waited until that first brick shattered the glass after 9/11. I should have recognized the issue during all those Middle Eastern jokes at our franchisees' expense. Instead, all I did was to ignore the jokes, my own cultural ignorance at work. Post 9/11, I decided to take that brick and make it my own personal spark.

As a CEO of 7-Eleven, my job was to protect all my employees and customers. If I had taken that responsibility literally, I would have just ordered more security guards for the stores and called it a day. But the brick through the window was my personal spark, and I was determined to learn more about the people who'd been the butt of so many jokes. What I found stunned me.

Our company, built on the entrepreneurial spirit of our franchisees, was a majority minority business. It was as if 7-Eleven had placed a job application station at Ellis Island, and thousands of Indians, Pakistanis, Swedes, Mexicans, and hundreds of other immigrants from countries throughout the world had signed up. I discovered that our franchisees and employees represented people from over 130 countries around the world. The very idea of this level of diversity that represented the global nature of 7-Eleven actually thrilled me, but now it was time for reflection. Why 7-Eleven? I began to ask why and traveled the country listening to their personal stories. In story after story, these multicultural 7-Eleven owners told me that they came to America believing in the American dream, a place where they could enjoy freedom while adding their cultural identity to the American quilt. Yet, too often they ran into that same brick of opposition.

Feeling this resistance to their own culture, these immigrants searched for a company that would allow them to have agency over their lives without having to deal with the racism. They looked for a role that would help them continue their culture of making family first, by hiring aunts, uncles, sons, and daughters to work the counter. They were continuing to develop their own cultural currency despite the obstacles placed in front of them. To these entrepreneurs, the 7-Eleven brand meant freedom—the true essence of American culture—their pathway to the American dream!

Now came the deep dive. I realized that 7-Eleven had become a conduit to a larger American dream for these immigrant families. They were willing to work hard, long hours in their stores. But they could see a payoff: It wasn't only the magic of 7-Eleven; the payoff was eventually having the economic power to create a next generation that didn't have to work behind a sales counter. I asked "why" even further, learning more about their hopes and dreams. What I discovered is that they also shared another common objective. They wanted their children to be college-educated lawyers, doctors, engineers, artists, or a thousand other opportunities that education would provide. Through the eyes of my first-generation franchisees, I saw that education *is* freedom. In this way, they were able to create opportunity, which allowed them to carve out their own version of the American dream for them and their families.

So, if you understood the cultural currency of that local 7-Eleven owner from India, or Egypt, or Saudi Arabia, who rang up your candy bars, gave you the weekly lottery tickets, or just said hello to you as you picked up your morning coffee, how could you ever throw bricks at them?

You couldn't. You wouldn't. The late Nobel Peace Prize winner John Hume reminded us, "Difference is the essence of humanity. Difference is an accident of birth, and it should therefore never be the source of hatred or conflict. The answer to difference is to respect it. Therein lies a most fundamental principle of peace: respect for diversity."

This same dynamic can play out in schools—that is, a lack of respect for diversity—and it's not just students. It's also teachers and administrators who may not take the time to learn about each student in their classrooms and instead rely upon stereotypes as a shortcut. They sometimes mistake a lack of English fluency for a lack of intelligence or hard work. Every time an immigrant student or an African-American student or a Latinx student is underestimated, an intellectual brick is being thrown at them.

This gets us to the second part of our cultural currency equation. Being aware of this knowledge isn't enough unless it's tied to action. Education without action is like buying a fishing pole without going to the lake to fish. To act with your cultural currency and to be effective, you need to do three specific things:

> The *first step* is to fight ignorance. Let's say that you decide that after the spark, reflection, and deep dive, to organize a Filipino Day at your school. Expect opposition. The opposition relies upon a collective ignorance to galvanize against a perceived threat. Fear is a great motivator, and what people without cultural literacy fear most is the unknown. Your goal is to not allow that opposition to stop you but instead aim to move them toward the yes versus the no. Yes to the idea. Yes to further exploration. Yes to continued growth.

> The *second step* is to embrace diversity. Diversity can be a word that means everything and nothing to people. It can be just a

bunch of ingredients that alone don't make much of anything. Or it can be an exciting gumbo. A gumbo brings together ingredients that wouldn't come together normally, and it is delicious. Embrace all the cultural currency you can; allow everyone to be seen and heard. And remember those loud and wrong ignorant people who used fear to oppose your ideas? Listen to them too. We can overcome cultural ignorance through exposure, education, and filling the vacuum of fear with knowledge. That bite of lumpia spring roll, the one that can create the spark, is still available to these people. Offer it to them, and then use your critical thinking skills and theirs to bring them along.

The *final step* is to be impactful, not performative. If you're gaining cultural currency daily, you are receiving something that is not only invaluable but that requires a reciprocal action just as valuable. What you contribute must reflect the value you gained. Too often, we as students, parents, and administrators go for the cheap expression of diversity versus the impactful. Saying that you respect Muslims is performative. Celebrating Eid al-Fitr (the festival at the end of Ramadan) with your Muslim students, teachers, and administrators is impactful. And what's even more impactful? Learning about how you can support your Muslim friends three hundred sixty-five days a year. Your goal is to make sure that everyone is seen, heard, and respected.

At 7-Eleven, I knew I couldn't just take the info I'd learned from the franchisees and do nothing. I had to use the power of the company to speak for those we hadn't spoken for in the past and to celebrate them in a way that would be a direct counter to the loudness of the bricks and the violence. I had to do my best to amplify and value the culture of our franchisees and what they represented to us and America. To begin, we threw a party—a party at Ellis Island where we celebrated the seventy-fifth anniversary of our founding. The symbolism of Ellis Island was about celebrating our diversity and the franchisees and licensees of over forty thousand stores worldwide. We wanted to let each of our employees, franchisees, and licensees know their valued their cultural contribution to the company. There was another bit of symbolism. This celebration happened in 2002, just one year after the terrorist attacks, and our event occurred within sight of the destroyed Twin Towers of the World Trade Center. We invited franchisees and employees from around the world, representing more than one hundred thirty different countries.

One story stood out. I brought a franchisee named Tariq Kahn to the stage. Tariq had come from Pakistan in 1979 with just a suitcase and $500 in his pocket. He'd arrived in New York City, found a beat-up old apartment on 110th and Broadway, one of those $50-a-night residence hotels, to start his life in America. Just down the hall from him lived a young Columbia graduate student who'd been unable to afford student housing. The student needed a place, anyplace, just to have a room to study and sleep. That Columbia student was me. We didn't meet during that time, but years later, Tariq would become the head of the National Coalition of Associations of 7-Eleven Franchisees (NCASEF), the group that represents franchise owners, and I would become CEO of 7-Eleven. We were two individuals living in the same space, at the same time, with the same objective and a similar outcome: achievement of the American dream. What are the odds? Once again, it became clear that our world is indeed very small.

Working closely with people from around the globe has given me a much greater appreciation for the value of cultural literacy. What unifies us is much more important than what divides us. Building your own cultural literacy is how you contribute to the fabric of the American dream. To develop this thoughtful exploration of others' hidden gifts, we can travel to a faraway land, experience different tastes and sounds, learn about unique and special histories, and find that the world can be quite small. In turn, you can reach out with the same thoughtful exploration to those in your own neighborhood. Unleash your curiosity and learn about their hidden gifts. As you partake in these exchanges, you will learn what so many have learned before: we are much more the same than we are different, but the unique gifts of others are often in those differences that we should celebrate.

CHAPTER 13

CHARACTER: YOU ARE WHAT YOU BELIEVE

"Character is like a tree and reputation like a shadow. The shadow is what we think of it; the tree is the real thing."

Abraham Lincoln

We have all heard the phrase "good character." From the time most of us were mere children, our parents, educators, and many people with whom we interacted reminded us of the importance of having good character in all that we do. Ideally, and in a perfect world, we work to form an identity that is representative of the highest and best qualities to ensure we live a life filled with integrity and strong morals. Sometimes, likely when we are much older, we determine if we have been successful in creating this so-called "good character." But how did we get there?

The question remains: Do we learn to build character over the course of our lives, or is it within our nature, something our parents gifted us in our DNA? The answer is likely a bit of both. Developing character is a lifelong ever-changing and ever-evolving journey. Without possessing certain elements of good character, it is nearly impossible to learn and to grow. So, it is essential that we understand what encompasses good character and how we can work each day to develop the elements and building blocks to create it.

Often, we take the word *character* for granted. Most of us wish to have the word ascribed to us, but few of us can define it. We can trace its origin back to the Greek character meaning an "engraved mark" or a "symbol or imprint on the soul." In ancient times, a character was the stamp or marking impressed into wax and clay. It was the signature or trademark thought to represent the individual and his identity. In many ways, that is still the case today.

By the seventeenth and eighteenth centuries, character became an important element of Western culture and society. Society spoke of people as having a strong or a weak character, a great deal of character, or no character at all. We encourage young people to develop their character and note that character is the most critical element on their path to adulthood. Character may lead to and shape your personality, but from the seventeenth century we know it as "the sum of qualities that defines a person." Such qualities may include our intellect, morality, judgment, attitude, and emotions.

These attributes will shape the way we see ourselves and the way others see us. The balance of these elements will shape the way we act and react to situations. They will ultimately affect our success or failure in life. They are also those attributes that make us unique from all other individuals in the world, almost like the very chains of DNA that form our molecular structure. These attributes produce something we think of as "self." The balance of these personal characteristics within the soul of everyone, and the way one prevails over others, is what makes each person's character unique and sets one individual apart from another. Our character becomes our identity, be it good or bad. Make no mistake about it, we can choose to shape our character and personality, thus empowering each of us to shape our lives.

FORM YOUR CHARACTER, SHAPE YOUR LIFE

Influenced by our environment or by those around us, it is unlikely that we inherit much of our character through our DNA. We learn good or bad behavior from others. As with other critical success factors we've explored, character mostly originates from within. This journey toward character development begins with a self-awareness and a belief that we can shape our own identity. We most easily accomplish this during our formative years, but anyone at any age can improve their character and reshape their identity. Scouting is an excellent example of the effort to mold a young person's character. The Boy Scout Law, learned by every young boy and girl in scouting, is defined by a desire to be "*trustworthy, loyal, helpful, friendly, courteous, kind, obedient, cheerful, thrifty, brave, clean, and reverent*." As a Scout myself, I can still recite these twelve attributes today. They have served me well.

The lessons I learned in scouting played a strong role in shaping my own character during my formative years. In fact, I had little awareness of the impact of these lessons until the Circle Ten Council in Texas asked me to deliver a speech on the topic of leadership to Scout leaders from across the country. While preparing for this speech, I pulled out my old *Boy Scout Handbook*. It was tattered and worn after surviving countless outings in my backpack as a child, but I was shocked at its relevance even today. The Scout motto is "Be Prepared." What better way to teach the importance of responding to change. The Scout slogan is "Do a Good Turn Daily!" What better way to foster selfless behavior that teaches us to be sensitive to others' needs.

When delivering the speech to this national group of Boy Scout leaders, I proudly acknowledged that after years of leadership training from Columbia Business School to the experience of leading two Fortune 500 corporations, my greatest lessons in leadership development came from that little green *Boy Scout Handbook*! I explained that the fundamentals learned in scouting provided a solid platform of personal values and leadership skill that I was able to build on throughout my career. This was not simply *learning* leadership from a book, but rather the ability to *practice* leadership through the experience of service as a patrol leader or senior patrol leader within a troop.

In that speech, I also explained that the same values and leadership skills were also highly influential forces in my pursuit of education. They contributed to my personal development in a variety of ways. They helped shape my identity and helped me develop a clear vision of the person I wanted to be. That person went to class "prepared." In the classroom, I was indeed trustworthy, loyal, helpful, friendly, courteous, kind, obedient, cheerful, thrifty, brave, clean, and reverent...or at least I tried! These attributes helped provide me a positive attitude toward my studies and likely contributed to a favorable impression on my teachers. Both resulted in a more productive learning experience. Character is, indeed, a critical element in education. My own character traits, developed from a young age, helped me thrive in the classroom and to welcome education as a crucial component of my own development.

Several core principles shape our character. These range from trust to integrity to awareness to persistence. It is possible, but unlikely, to build good character while missing even one of these. However, something remarkable occurs when you hone in on the best of each, recognizing that they will be integral parts of who you are. To that end, let's unpack each in greater detail.

INTEGRITY: WHERE IT ALL BEGINS

If we are to build youth of strong character, it is only natural that we recognize the components that comprise character. Integrity, a word that we are all familiar with, is often the prerequisite for any person of good character. Simply put, it is rare to find someone who has character without integrity. The Boy Scout Law begins with the concept of being "trustworthy," likely because it is a cornerstone of good character. We must trust and be trusted to become effective in influencing others and leading an integrity-filled life. The same is true in any educational environment. The ability to develop intellectual honesty and personal integrity are integral aspects of learning, leading, and teaching others. If we aren't honest with ourselves, we can't be honest with others. Honesty requires an open mind and a willingness to accept divergent points of view, to dissect those opinions and to learn from them.

It takes an open mind to create intellectual honesty. It requires each of us to explore all sides of an issue and to understand another's point of view. The concept of intellectual honesty is something that feels lost in today's hectic political world. An iconic meme has been making the rounds of the internet, showing two people observing a number from different sides. From one side it appears to be a nine and from the other side appears as a six. Both people are correct in their view because of their unique perspective. To reconcile this difference, do they agree to see the number from each other's perspective or do they lock down on their point of view with militant ignorance? This ability to understand the various sides of an issue or perspectives is often lost in the emotion of a debate. Intellectual honesty is the relentless pursuit of truth even if that truth conflicts with our preconceived notions or, even more harrowing, our personal values or ideology.

Just think of how far we would get together, as a team, or as a planet, if we recognized that two people can look at the same problem yet solve it in different ways. We impart our opinions as facts and find it insulting when another doesn't see things the way we do. That is, at least in part, because we are not demonstrating integrity in our interactions, but also because we may be so arrogant that we believe what we see is the only reality that matters. The truth couldn't be further from that. Life is for interpretation. The only absolute is that your paradigms and worldview will often differ from that of your neighbor's.

HUMILITY:
REMAIN HUMBLE AND WELCOME THE THOUGHTS OF OTHERS

Humility, then, helps us recognize that our belief system matters, but so does the belief system of others. Humility is what clearly defines the line between confidence and arrogance. To be confident is to know what we *don't* know but also to know that we can find the answer. Humility means "the state of being humble," originating in the Latin word *humilis,* meaning "low." This can be confusing because the pure definition of humility might be read as the "state of being low." While technically correct, the more appropriate definition is "the absence of pride or arrogance."

Humility is best defined as the state of understanding that one has more to learn. While we can have confidence in our ability to learn, we must always acknowledge that we don't know it all. We can take pride in our accomplishments but must be careful that our pride doesn't define us. Even the Bible references the importance of humility. Proverbs 11:2 says, "When pride comes, then comes disgrace, but with humility comes wisdom" (NIV). This appropriate balance of confidence with humility will contribute to our character and lead to a successful future.

The need to be thankful, then, goes hand in hand with the importance of humility. An important element of character development is recognizing that others are instrumental our success. Michelle Obama said it well when she stated, "We learned about gratitude and humility—that so many people had a hand in our success, from the teachers who inspired us to the janitors who kept our school clean... and we were taught to value everyone's contribution and treat everyone with respect." It could be a teacher, a mentor, a coworker, or a boss, but our success is so often dependent on learning and support from those around us. We remain grounded when we facilitate an awareness of the importance of others and the role that they've played in our lives.

GRATITUDE: BE THANKFUL FOR LIFE'S GIFTS

Being thankful for what we have is often undermined by negative feelings or dissatisfaction with our current situation. If you hate school, you're unlikely to be successful at your schoolwork. If you hate your job, you're unlikely to perform above your peers. Dr. Kerry Howells teaches educational philosophy at the University of Tasmania in Australia. She noticed that most of her students were complaining about what they didn't have or what they weren't getting from their classroom experience. They were not "engaged," and a student who is not engaged will not be an effective learner. While complaining about the system being rigged against them, they were not recognizing that their very resentment was undermining their ability to be engaged, and, hence, compromised their ability to learn.

"Without much preconceived intention at the time," she said, "I suggested that perhaps gratitude could be a valuable alternative paradigm to the one of resentment that predominated. Without much prompting on my part, many students started to approach their studies with more gratitude. They reported that when they practiced more gratitude when they studied, they experienced increased engagement, greater connection to the subject and teacher, a deeper understanding of content, and increased motivation." The education value of gratitude then became her imperative. She has since taught the relationship between gratitude and student engagement.

You may not know how to express or even feel gratitude. For many of us, it is not top of mind.

Practicing mindfulness is one way to do this. At least once a day, sit quietly and think through a few things for which you are grateful. Create a mental image and let the feeling of gratitude permeate your mind and your body. Doing this every day will help require your brain to be naturally more grateful. After every session, you will begin to feel happier. Research has shown that it takes only a few weeks of gratitude practice for people to start showing different brain patterns that lead to greater empathy and happiness. Training your brain to feel more gratitude will improve your sense of humility, compassion, empathy, and overall contentment, leading to a strong character. Reprogramming your brain is more than just thinking, it is also doing. Beyond simple meditation, we must take actions that express our gratitude by serving others, giving up our personal prejudice, giving back, saying sorry, and letting go.

In other words, it isn't just the thoughts of gratitude but also the deeds of gratitude that count. Given the many benefits and the strong contribution to your character, why not practice it? It will get easier over time. Many studies have found that people who consciously count their blessings tend to be happier and less depressed. Gratitude goes hand in hand with success. If you are grateful to learn or to work, then an air of contentment will envelop you in everything you do. It will be an infectious level of happiness that others will notice and hopefully adopt. Ralph Waldo Emerson said, "Cultivate the habit of being grateful for every good thing that comes to you, and to give thanks continuously. And because all things have contributed to your advancement, you should include all things in your gratitude."

WAKING UP: OPENING YOUR EYES TO THE WORLD AROUND YOU

Building good character is not an act that occurs overnight. It takes time, energy, and a relentless dedication to doing the right thing. Above and beyond that, it also requires that we maintain an awareness of what is going on around us. As Americans, we accept a responsibility to stand against oppression and violation of civil rights. We see the responsibility to defend this right as part of our American character. Our Declaration of Independence upholds the principle that all men are created equal and the U.S. Constitution gives us equal protection under the law. Together, as Americans, we are only as strong as the sum of our parts and, therefore, must be able to embrace differences in culture, customs, religion, or appearance to protect our own rights and the rights of others.

In recent times, however, the idea that we are better together has not been apparent in our collective behavior. An expression once used to foster cultural awareness has re-emerged: *woke*. This concept is not new. The phrase "stay woke" has been present in African-American vernacular since the 1930s. The original intention of the expression meant to be informed, educated, and conscious of social injustice or racial inequity. This, of course, should be a good thing. However, what started as a movement to recognize injustice has now become a politically divisive and racially charged concept. Sadly, the concept of *woke* became associated with violence and civil disobedience. In the wake of several police shootings and fueled by the universal frustration over COVID lockdowns, the summer of 2020 erupted in violence as the Black Lives Matter movement embraced the idea of *woke*. Those opposed to their stance turned *woke* into an affront. The original intention of *woke* to perpetuate civility was ultimately perceived to be not civil at all. What began as a positive, a way of referencing one's empathy and sensitivity, eventually became perceived by some as a personal affront to others. In some incomprehensible way, it became an expression of reverse discrimination.

The result was polarizing. Suddenly, the spirit of *woke* became highjacked by both right and left to express outrage at the other's behavior. If we explore the root cause of this polarization, we will find commonality. Those who disdain the concept, fear the civil disobedience that they believe the Black Lives Matter movement triggered. Those who embraced the concept fear continued inequity in policing. What began as a fear of pervasive racism on one side became also a fear of reverse discrimination on the other. The *woke* vernacular quickly took on a life of its own, expanding beyond racial issues to a host of other social fears. How ironic, since the original intent of "*stay woke*" going back to the 1930s was to celebrate openness, awareness, and acceptance of others. At the heart of that acceptance is the ability to overcome fear. As organic creatures, we are susceptible to the fight or flight instincts that make us size up others and determine quickly (often based on physical appearance) if they are friend or foe. It is natural to perceive that someone who looks like us and acts like us will present no threat.

While fear can be a natural reaction, we must learn to rise above it. Racism in all forms is rooted in fear causing distrust and hatred. But fear can be managed, and trust of others can be learned. For trust to be learned and for us to overcome all forms of interpersonal fear, we must learn another essential element of character: forgiveness. In moments of fear, we lose our good character, turning to judgment and hatred instead. To most, this is an unconscious act.

At some point in our life, we will be hurt by someone or something. As with any form of adversity, it is not the pain that matters but rather our reaction to that pain. The natural instinct of anger and revenge will often hurt us more than our enemy. Forgiveness isn't easy, but it is a prerequisite for trust. As humans, we are flawed. It is only natural that each of us will fail in the eyes of our friends, family, or even our God at one time or another. Reconciliation requires us, as individuals, to forgive and to be forgiven. We carry a grudge without forgiveness, and that negativity affects us more than it affects the ones we haven't forgiven. Only through forgiveness can we learn to trust again. Only through forgiveness can we rise above our own intolerance. Only through forgiveness can we rise above fear. Forgiveness is an essential quality of good character as it allows us to extinguish the fire that can eventually consume us.

COMMUNITY: A SENSE OF PURPOSE IN SHARING

Ultimately, the antidote to social division of any type is for each of us to learn both acceptance and compassion. Compassion is the ability to understand others and to suppress our instinct to be judgmental. Everyone has issues. The person who disappoints us may have a horrible backstory that could be contributing to their negative behavior. They may have lost a family member or perhaps were recently diagnosed with a terminal illness. Without a window into the hearts and minds of others, it is impossible to know their pain. Compassion is the ability to understand and to have empathy for others who may be less fortunate or who may have issues affecting their behavior. Compassion can help us learn. By understanding others, we better understand ourselves.

Only through forgiveness and compassion can we practice another essential element of character: community. We can characterize community as seeking the greater good for the whole over the individual. I'm a capitalist. I believe in the ability for one to exercise self-determination and to translate hard work into success. I also believe in the obligation, as a member of the community and a citizen of the world, to always seek the greater good. While some see these two concepts as being in conflict, they can be quite complementary.

Some may look at corporate involvement in social causes as a sign of weakness. Companies or executives may be accused of *virtue signaling*. Instead, here is a way to see corporate involvement in social issues as a strength. Corporations are the ultimate instrument of capitalism. One of the fundamentals of capitalism is the need to grow shareholder value. That only happens through attention to the stakeholders: customers, employees, and ultimately shareholders. We sometimes forget that a company's stakeholders represent a cross-section of society. Therefore, anything we do to help even a subset of customers, employees, and even shareholders is intended to benefit all stakeholders in the enterprise. Take care of stakeholders, and shareholder value will take care of itself.

At times, a corporation's appeal to one subset of society can create conflict by offending another. We've seen companies be "cancelled" by some who disagree with their actions. The irony is that such actions are almost always grounded in the fundamentals of capitalism, as a corporation strives to accomplish the difficult task of satisfying all stakeholders. Rather than penalize corporations engaging in social good, we should find ways to understand the purpose behind those efforts. Balancing the risk of political fallout should not outweigh the need to be responsive to customers and employees. The ability to improve shareholder value and to champion social good should not be mutually exclusive.

It was this sense of purpose, for example, that inspired the Education is Freedom Foundation. Like any corporation, 7-Eleven and Blockbuster depended heavily on a quality, educated workforce. Public schools are the fertile fields for growing these workers. Why not then invest in them by providing a path to a better education? The more spent on building quality employees, the lower the turnover and the higher the customer service. All of this contributes to improved sales and profits, resulting in higher shareholder value. The common good and shareholder value are clearly not mutually exclusive principles. They can be accomplished in harmony.

PERSISTENCE AND DETERMINATION ARE OMNIPOTENT

A final element of good character is integral to one's success. Persistence and determination, in the words of Calvin Coolidge, are omnipotent. "Press on," he said. "Nothing in the world can take the place of persistence. Talent will not; nothing is more common than unsuccessful men with talent. Genius will not; unrewarded genius is almost a proverb. Education will not; the world is full of educated derelicts. Persistence and determination alone are omnipotent."

Have you ever noticed that people who are determined, people who are persistent, people who never give up all have a common characteristic? They're happy. They may be obsessed with their focus on success. They may be working harder than anyone around them, but they are happy. They are happy because they see the opportunity before them, and they are grateful for it. While working at McDonald's—my first job during high school—I saw the Calvin Coolidge quote on a poster. I admired Ray Kroc for what he had created in the growing McDonald's hamburger chain. If Ray Kroc thought this quote was important enough to warrant a posting in every one of his McDonald's restaurants, then it must be important to me and my life, I thought.

So, I took the advice literally and began to approach my work with a different level of determination. When a manager asked me to clean the grill, I did it with determination. When asked to clean the parking lot, persistence made me run, not walk, to clean up to two hundred yards in each direction of the store. One day, when the manager removed my favorite poster from the break-room, I asked if I could take it home. The quote was powerful, and I felt it held a secret to success. I wanted to preserve it in a special way. So, I took it to high school shop class, mounted it on a board, and stained and distressed it to make it look old. I then proudly displayed the new "plaque" on my desk as a form of inspiration when studying. The plaque stayed with me through high school, college, and grad school and accompanied me to my office at my first professional job. It has been with me since high school and today still decorates my desk today.

Shortly after being recognized by the Horatio Alger Association of Distinguished Americans, I received a note of congratulations from Warren Buffett along with a copy of his autobiography. I was honored and delighted. As I read his story of success, one chapter stopped me in my tracks. There it was, an entire chapter, dedicated to the simple one-page quote by Calvin Coolidge. The page was identical to my McDonald's poster, even the same font! A coincidence? I think not. I can't stress enough, and I'm sure Warren Buffett will agree, that persistence and determination indeed *are* omnipotent!

BUILD YOUR CHARACTER NOW!

It is never too late to build good character. It is a work in progress from birth. It is etched into our very being and becomes our identity. We can let others influence that character, or we can establish our own identity and strive to build character in a way that allows us to make a favorable mark on the world. Many things can shape your character for better and for worse—the circumstance into which you were born; the friends and family influences during your formative years; your religious and academic education, and so on. Tragedy, disease, or abuse can all impact your character. Such life-shaping influences may make you bitter and resentful or hopeful and grateful. As with all response to change as earlier referenced, it is not the change that matters, but your response to that change will determine your character and define your identity.

This makes it even more essential, therefore, for each of us to strive to improve our self-awareness and to initiate our own "self-study" in the lifelong journey of character development.

It takes a tremendous level of discipline to dedicate yourself to success in your educational journey. As such, it is no coincidence that successful students often turn into men and women of high character. It is also no coincidence that those who continue to improve their character become the leaders of our society, the game-changers in this world, and the luminaries that shape our very future.

SECTION V
LEARNING TO LIVE

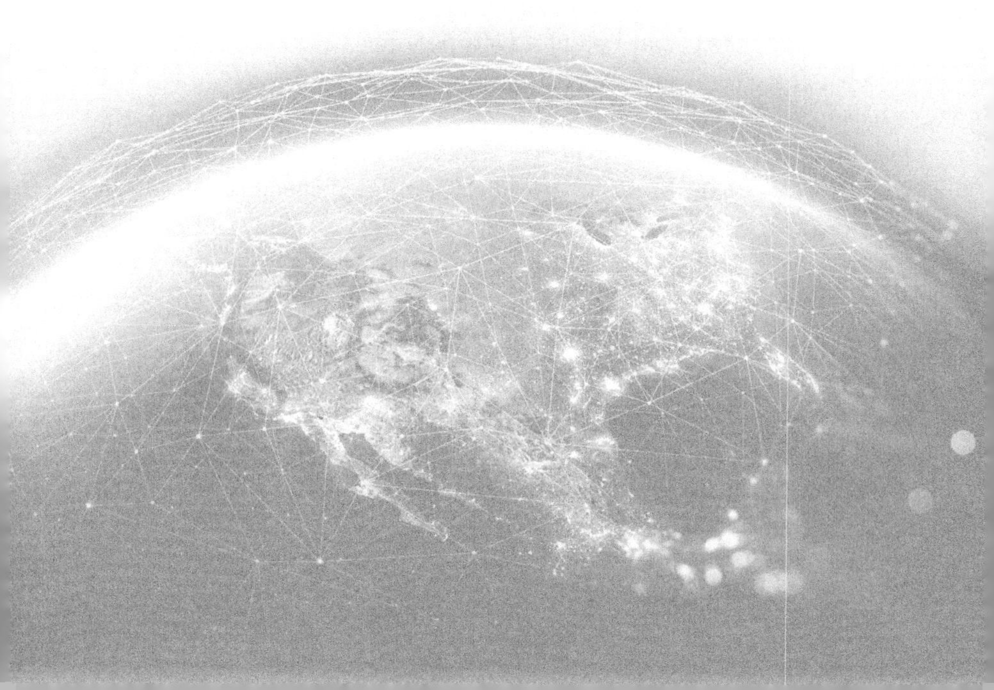

Each of the previous chapters addressed critical factors in navigating a successful pathway to education. Within each, we see real examples of unlocking the doors to learning. We also see the importance of personal initiatives and how owning these core concepts can transform our present and future lives.

While these attributes may individually serve as a tool, they are collectively a road map that will guide each of us through a journey of lifelong learning. As with any set of steps, the road map works best through the collective strength of the combination of all nine critical success factors. Now that we have explored each of them individually, let's see how they all come together to create a personal road map for successful navigation of one's learning and perhaps one's life.

Change happens. Most important is to remember that it's not about "what" happened to us, but rather the "way" we respond to any given change that will matter. Change was a given in my career. It is part of the daily reality in everyone's life. My ability to manage that change made me a better leader.

Confidence was and continues to be a driving force in my commitment to lifelong learning. I believe I can do anything, given enough time and effort. Can I paint a picture, write a song, erect a building, change career, learn a new language? The answer is yes to all. Yes, I can. As my friend Adan Gonzalez says, "*Sí, se puede*." Though not a direct translation, the expression means "yes, it is possible."

The pursuit of *clarity* can often be most challenging because the most difficult task in the world is taking the highly complex and making it simple. It doesn't have to be that way. Anyone can do this. It is a matter of focus and discipline to simplify the process of both receiving and giving information.

Critical thinking is what helps us to learn. It causes us to question the "what," "why," and "how" of any situation and to build knowledge by constantly searching for more and better information to ultimately make the most informed decision.

Curiosity is a driving force in allowing us to deal with change. If we believe in the power of curiosity, it can make us anxious to see what was on the other side of any dark cloud. Unleash your inner child to ask "why."

But curiosity alone is sometimes useless without *creativity*. The two go hand in hand. Finding creative solutions can occur only with a curious mind, and a curious mind is a creative mind. Creativity, is indeed, knowledge having fun.

Working effectively with others happens only through *collaboration*. The benefits of collaboration occur when we realize that we have much to learn from others. Simply put, together is better!

If we reflect upon the many cultures and interests that make up this wonderful world in which we live, we will recognize that *cultural literacy* allows us to relate to any individual, anywhere in this world.

Acceptance and appreciation of others cannot occur without strong *character*. Our individual character is made up of those characteristics that will set us apart from the rest. It is, indeed, our identity that will follow us through life's journey and help others choose to be a part of our success or failure.

This is the road map. If you can dream it, you can achieve it with these nine qualities.

In this last section of the book, "Learning to Live," we will explore how these concepts will help you individually while helping our collective society empower a brighter future through knowledge. Together we will explore the role of technology as a great enabler, exponentially improving the accessibility and availability of learning tools. We will celebrate the joy of lifelong learning as a pathway to the richness of life. Finally, we will draw the distinction between knowledge and wisdom to show how our individual and collective wisdom can be the Rx for humanity.

Once we begin living to learn, only then can we learn to live!

CHAPTER 14

TECHNOLOGY: THE GREAT ENABLER

"As technology breaks down the physical barriers of college campuses, the extraordinary intellectual capital of the educator community is becoming available to anyone committed to learning—regardless of age, income or location."

Laura Arrillaga-Andreessen

Technology is changing the way we teach and the way we learn. New inventions have always enabled education, but our innovations still required intervention to help us learn. A book made it possible to read about any given subject, but it could not answer questions or allow the user to dig deeper into any one paragraph or chapter. This required the intervention of a teacher or tutor to facilitate the exploration process of learning and to guide you to needed information.

The ability to *Ask Siri*, *Google* a question, or use *Wikipedia* for deeper knowledge of any given subject are just the beginning of a coming revolution in technology. New technologies such as virtual reality or artificial intelligence can take any learning experience one step further. Compare the traditional biology textbook that lets you see the schematic of human anatomy versus watching an autopsy being performed with your virtual reality goggles. Consider the opportunity to improve your study of the Japanese language by using the translate feature on Facebook to communicate with a new friend from Tokyo. They learn English while you learn Japanese, and you both make a new friend and have fun learning a new language.

The use of technology to advance knowledge is not new. Since early human beings, we have relied on breakthroughs in various forms of technology to help us learn. The Chinese are credited with developing early forms of printing more than two thousand years ago, but Johannes Gutenberg, the German inventor known for creating the first printing press using movable type, kicked off the age of print. In the late 1790s, the printing method of lithography began the use of chemical processing that led to offset printing, making it possible to mass produce books. It's hard to imagine being able to learn over the past two hundred years without access to textbooks.

In 1801, the inventor James Pillans invented the first chalkboard or "blackboard" to better teach his students at a high school in Edinburgh, Scotland. Around the same time, in 1795, Nicolas-Jacques Conté invented the modern pencil. While versions of the pencil go back hundreds of years, this scientist in Napoleon Bonaparte's army created the modern graphite pencil that wasn't mass produced until the 1900s.

In the mid-1950s, two inventions improved the classroom. Overhead projectors were used during WWII for mission briefings, but a 3M employee named Roger Appeldorn created a transparent film and the overhead projectors that were used in classrooms for decades. Also in the 1950s, an inventor named Chester Carlson wanted to create an easier way to make carbon copies. He perfected electrophotography, which led to the development of the first photocopy machines.

Not until the mid-1960s did Texas Instruments introduce the handheld calculator. The HP 12C by Hewlett-Packard was an essential tool for most business applications that I continue to carry today. That same technology is now available as an application on the iPhone. When Adam Osborne and Lee Felsenstein designed the first portable computer in 1981, it wasn't exactly a laptop, but at about twenty-five pounds, the Osborne 1 was known as the first "portable" computer.

These innovations advanced the ability to teach and learn, but not until about 1990 did Tim Berners-Lee, a British scientist, create the World Wide Web to enable information sharing between scientists and academics. Combine that interconnectivity with Wi-Fi communications ability and put that connectivity into a handheld device, and we have suddenly created the capacity to provide more information in the palm of your hand than exists in all the books in the Library of Congress.

An ancient proverb that has both Hebrew and Chinese attribution says, "Do not confine your children to your own learning, for they were born in another time." This is indeed another time! Today, the explosion of technology has created opportunities that few of us can even imagine.

WHERE ARE WE HEADED? TECH INSIDE THE CLASSROOM AND OUTSIDE THE CLASSROOM

Technology may indeed be the key to addressing the worldwide challenge of education. The pandemic created awareness and an urgent need for technology to replace the ability to teach in a classroom for extended periods. The silver cloud of this disruption was threefold. It accelerated deployment of Wi-Fi and electronic devices to even the most underprivileged. It prompted the accelerated development of online curriculums and learning tools. Perhaps most importantly, it demonstrated the power of technology to help transform education. While we are in the very early stage of this transformation, the opportunities are endless. Several critical elements in technology will change everything.

The first is *access*. Lower cost of hardware, availability of new software, and ubiquitous access to Wi-Fi will eventually be a reality worldwide thanks to rapid breakthroughs in the commercial space that will make affordable global access a reality.

When the pandemic forced schools across the country to pivot to remote learning, the depth of the digital divide in our country was laid bare. In Texas alone, we discovered that 1.8 million public school students from kindergarten through twelfth grade did not have Wi-Fi connectivity at home. One out of every four students did not have a computer or tablet to access online learning. Federal and state governments, along with corporations like AT&T, stepped up to provide hardware, hotspots, and many other resources to allow for access to the online instruction so desperately needed during the shutdown. This crisis, while temporarily solved with interim solutions such as a hotspot versus robust access to Wi-Fi 6 streaming capability, has also sparked an awareness of the opportunity and a passion for the solution. Across the country, corporations are working on virtual learning software and hardware at a pace previously unseen. We are on the cusp of a transformation greater than any ever witnessed in education. The greater the access and options we offer, the higher likelihood they will be used to improve learning.

While technology has, in the past few years, been accused of worsening the socioeconomic divide, this crisis has accelerated the steps necessary to close that gap through education. It would have taken our country up to twenty years to accomplish universal streaming access and to make hardware and software education available to all. This acceleration, forced upon us by the pandemic, put hardware and software tools in the hands of all students at a rate we have never seen. Post-pandemic, these technologies remain available as a valuable desktop tool to enhance learning in the classroom or at home, serving as a portal to learning that we've never previously enjoyed. Technology could indeed become the great enabler.

A second critical element in technology that will change the future of education is *artificial intelligence* that will transform the teaching and learning process. The fundamental premise of artificial intelligence is that machine learning will allow machines (computers) to process massive amounts of information faster and faster, replicating our human learning process but doing so with unimaginable speed. In the same fashion, artificial intelligence will help humans access and process massive amounts of information more quickly. The technology can anticipate our learning needs, tailoring curriculums to the way we learn and the speed at which we learn.

Artificial intelligence may become the key to personalized, collaborative, and peer-to-peer learning for students. We all learn at different rates and in different ways. With AI tools, a teacher can modify instruction to adapt to the unique learning capabilities of individual students. Even the role of the teacher is likely to change, with teachers shifting to more counseling and advising while learning becomes more of a self-starting initiative by the student. An individual engaged in online learning will be able to have the teaching style modified based on interactive teaching, testing, teaching again, and retesting as the machine learns in real time which approaches the student is best absorbing. One might imagine a teacher serving in the capacity of a concierge, directing each student to a particular curriculum and potentially to a best-of-class online professor. Using the latest technology, the content and teaching methods can be curated to present those proven to be most successful in helping that individual student to learn. The role of teacher, then, could potentially evolve into more of a coach, directing students to the path that will give them the best results.

A third opportunity of technology is the use of *blockchain* to enable many aspects of student interaction. A company in Dallas called GreenLight Credentials, for example, pioneered the use of secure blockchain storage capabilities to manage the traditionally challenging area of student transcripts. Student record keeping has always been a challenge due to privacy concerns and protections of the student and parents.

Recording test scores and grades have been the purview of individual schools with a mixed bag of procedures from paper to electronic capture. Transfer of this information has always been a problem, making it more difficult for the student to communicate critical result information to colleges and potential employers. By using a blockchain secured account for record keeping, students can now collect transcript information from multiple schools or classes, store these records in a safe environment, and safely make that information available to other schools and potential employers. This technology makes it much easier for employers to review transcripts and offer employment to students without trespassing on privacy concerns. Today, when most people think of blockchain, they think of cryptocurrency. Yes, crypto was the first practical application to scale up the use of blockchain technology, but there are so many more reasons (like transcripts or even micro learning grants) to embrace this approach to protecting secure information.

Here is another idea that I've been exploring and trying to advance: think about the potential for micro scholarships to be granted *before* not *after* a student has had academic success. During the pandemic, we saw students use their digital classroom tools diligently but without enthusiasm. Once finishing their schoolwork, many would take the same device and joyfully play video games for hours on end. One difference in these two applications of technology was the availability of incentives. The ability to win points, badges, or even a hat for your avatar are incentives that hook the child into continued play. This is the spirit of micro scholarships, to bring incentives to the students so that they can earn something more valuable than game points. With micro scholarships, they can be earning while learning their way to a quality education.

Using today's technology, we can offer micro-scholarship rewards in as little as twenty-cent increments that accumulate over time in a blockchain secured account. Imagine a student earning enough "scholar dollars" for a full college scholarship by the time they become a high school senior. A company like American Airlines could provide fifty cents to a student who passes a geography test as they learn STEAM and hope to become a future pilot. Imagine a sophomore in high school with an account that has a balance of $20,000 earned twenty cents at a time toward tuition and books at the college of their choice. Imagine the ability of Khan Academy to reward successful completion of a mathematics module with a small learning grant from the services firm Deloitte, to encourage the young student to learn accounting. Imagine a world where parents are encouraging their children to put down their schoolwork because they've been too absorbed in learning!

All of this and more is possible through creative applications of technology to encourage focus and engagement. One thing is certain, the future of education technology will be as disruptive to traditional education as the internet has been for retailing or electric vehicles have been to the traditional automotive industry. What was once a future vision is now here for all to embrace.

THE BENEFITS OF A TECHNOLOGICALLY ADVANCED CLASSROOM

Now is the time to reimagine education nationally, bringing together the for-profit and nonprofit sectors in a common effort to create a better way to learn. School districts have scrambled with public and private support to offer software, connectivity, and devices to those in need. In many cases, temporary solutions were the most realistic, using off the shelf software from multiple sources since there was little time for customization. Inevitably, remote learning has presented challenges for teachers, students, and parents. If technology is the great enabler that can re-energize education by putting the keys to an unlimited learning in the hands of every child, then why are so many struggling? Attendance has suffered, grades are measurably declining, and many are longing for a return to classroom normalcy.

We put digital tools in place, but today these tools lack the integration and capacity for engagement that are necessary to make virtual learning transformative. Today's online classrooms provide tools but not solutions. To date, we have simply made it possible to go online and learn in the way we've taught for hundreds of years. Instead of simply creating video access to a teacher and a blackboard in the traditional sense, education needs to become a dynamic, engaging experience. Instead of looking at this as a temporary fix, we should see it as an unprecedented opportunity that can—and must—catapult us to create a world-class virtual learning system of the future.

Step one in this education technology revolution must be integration. The tools exist, but we have not yet unleashed the power of technology by strategically integrating or reimagining how to use them. For example, teachers today may use software like Google Classroom or PowerSchool, but because these are discrete software solutions that don't allow for smooth integration, an ineffective and intimidating experience can result. Remember the days before Microsoft Office, when word processing, spreadsheets, or presentations were all separate applications? This is the reality of academic software solutions today. Software integration isn't only needed for core curriculums but could also provide important linkages to third-party providers. Links to college courses can allow high school students to build credits online. Linkage to corporations can facilitate internships, part-time employment, or even full-time jobs. Imagine a student earning an internship at NASA, where her resume would then reside online and potentially lead to a full-time job in the aerospace industry. All of this is possible through technology.

Step two is to make these tools more engaging. Why is it that a student may passively interact with a one-dimensional class online and then use that same device to become actively immersed in a video game for hours? In the former scenario, knowledge is being transmitted from the teacher to the students. Instead, imagine an interactive experience where technology can be used to bring students into a virtual boardroom, operating room, or laboratory as real-life actions are unfolding. The practical applications of this new model for education are unlimited. We can create a more compelling way to learn, with images, not just words, and with experiences and active participation instead of just receiving information. In our technology-enabled world, learning could become more engaging than your favorite video game while creating a sense of community through virtual participation with friends. Imagine a student in premed being able to "level-up" through graduate school chemistry. If we applied the same gamification creativity to the educational experience, we could achieve even higher levels of engagement.

As the beneficiaries of an educated workforce, every corporation and small business should see this as a worthwhile investment. The opportunity is here today for corporations to demonstrate that shareholder value and social good are not mutually exclusive principles. Since the single greatest demand for an educated workforce is the corporate world, it's time for corporations to invest in our students by funding the technology available today to create a better-educated society. If we can shift our lens to look at technology as an enabler, we can use the power of these new tools to create more informed students, a stronger pipeline for future employment, and communities where the socioeconomic divide diminishes exponentially. The time is now to create a portal for all students to have access to unlimited learning. The impact, not just on education but on the world at large, will be felt in ways we never dreamed possible.

ENABLING US ALL

With the idea that technology is going to shrink the world, will it provide greater access to education for underserved communities? If so, how? What will this shift in tech education accomplish for these communities? How will they have greater access? What will be the collective benefits? If technology is the great enabler, will it be a great savior as well?

As with any new technology, neither the benefits nor the applications will be immediately apparent; people are often limited to what they see today, unable to see what's possible tomorrow. When Tesla transformed the concept of electric vehicles, our imaginations didn't immediately leap to autonomous vehicles. As we looked into the future and began to understand the power of 5G wireless communications, the evolution of electric vehicles to autonomous, driverless capability became a reality, but that vision had little or nothing to do with batteries. The point? Technology available today will not help us envision the impact on teaching and learning tomorrow; instead, that vision will evolve over time. One thing is certain: the access to information available to anyone with an electronic device and connectivity is unprecedented.

The number of smartphone users reached 5.22 billion by the end of 2020, which represents 66 percent of the world's population. In 2022, the number of global smartphone users was estimated at 6.6 billion and was forecasted to reach 6.8 billion by 2023. With a global population of eight billion, 85 percent of the world's people will own or possess a smartphone. While it is anything but the ideal teaching device, it is an important step in providing access. Through that simple device, any individual anywhere in the world has a portal to unlimited learning. Yes, the content must be improved and integrated. Yes, the access to Wi-Fi or cellular connectivity must improve. Yes, the devices to access that connectivity must become more sophisticated. All these steps will occur in the next decade, but we should all recognize that a game-changing tool is now in the hands of nearly 85 percent of the world's population. With that recognition, we should begin to improve the software and hardware necessary to make that accessibility truly a portal to unlimited learning.

Will this access change the world? Most certainly. Just as the modern printing press made it possible to print books, that technology didn't immediately transform third world countries. But just as visionaries like Bob Brown and Oprah Winfrey made books available to children in Africa who would not have otherwise had access, the future power of technology will light up the far corners of the world where poverty and illiteracy stem from lack of access, not intellect.

Still, that is the future, but what about today? That is a description of what's possible for them; but what about you? If you believe that education *is* freedom, if you believe that knowledge can shape your destiny, then the tools for access to that knowledge, the tools to shape your own destiny are available today. The power of tomorrow's technology is in your hands today.

An example of this potential is the story of William Talley. Growing up in southern Illinois, William is as American as the soil his family shaped into a vocation. His mother, Sarah Frey, did it the hard way. Watching her family's humble farm about to be broken up and sold, she jumped in with her own version of the C-Suite Learnings. Sarah had to deal with change and adversity from the time she was born. One of twenty-seven siblings (literally), she had no time for self-pity. She accepted her personal adversity and saw it as a strength. When the family farm was on the verge of failure, she stepped in and convinced a local bank to help her acquire it. She embraced change. She had the confidence to walk into a newly built Walmart distribution center and pitch her watermelon and pumpkin business.

The clarity of her plan sold the executives on the idea that she could do it. Still, it took curiosity to learn the ropes of the complex Walmart system and creativity to find solutions that had her lining up trucks and product to fill their orders. It took collaboration for her to pull together the many growers and drivers needed to make this happen. Her cultural literacy enables Sarah to move comfortably in all circles. Finally, the strength of Sarah Frey's character made people want to trust her and help her succeed. Today, Frey leads one of the largest privately held produce operations in the country. Would she say that education is freedom? Absolutely. While her formal education was carved out of an Illinois rural public school system and Frontier Community College, she is a Harvard case study (literally) in business acumen. Frey beat the odds. She is an entrepreneur whose success came down to persistence, determination, and a hard-fought education through experience. For her two young boys, Frey wanted a different path. She encouraged them to study hard and find an easier way to success through a quality education.

Her son William Talley had a different idea. Watching his mom succeed through grit and determination, he believed that he could do the same and that school was not a priority. Many of his classmates were content to satisfy the minimum requirements of school and to join their family on the farm. It is, most certainly, a noble and highly respected profession. William felt that school was boring and a waste of time. He enjoyed learning but didn't like taking classes. He loved history and was good at math, but he couldn't care less about the things that took place inside the classroom.

Then a transformation occurred. William discovered the power of YouTube to make history come alive. His mom scolded him for too much screen time, but he was devouring history online. Textbook history was dull and uninspiring, but watching YouTube videos of World War II was a different story.

Meanwhile, textbook math was dull at best, but William discovered the secret weapon of Khan Academy math online to help him practice and make the difficult seem simple. No one forced him to adopt the power of technology to transform his education process. He did this on his own. He realized that he could tailor his education to the tools and processes that worked for him. Did he still need to pass his high school tests and prepare for the SAT? Of course, but he did it with a secret weapon at his fingertips. He unlocked the power of technology to ignite his curiosity and supplement his formal classroom studies.

The result: William went from a B-/C+ student in grammar school to achieving more than a 4.0 in high school while completing more than forty hours of early college credits at the same time! This is the power of technology. William now embraces learning, but the power of technology made his education come alive and propelled his success in high school. William was recently accepted at Harvard for the class of 2027 and will begin his college journey there this fall.

The secret to unlocking the technology that is available today is to use the road map outlined in this book! Accept the *change*. Technology is indeed an enabler, but it is a double-edged sword. It can increase the digital divide, or it can slam that divide shut through self-determination. If a child can't learn the way we teach, technology will allow us to teach the way they learn! It takes *confidence* to take the initiative to use the tools available to us. If we are unafraid of technology, we can use the new tools to cut through the clutter of information to *clarify* and simplify. Technology will stimulate curiosity because the entire universe is accessible with a few keystrokes.

The power of technology enables *critical thinking*. It takes a dose of *curiosity* and a little *creativity* to explore this universe of data, but those attributes have never been more easily executed than via today's technology. When it comes to *collaboration*, the World Wide Web is the ideal tool. On the internet, there may be no better example than *Wikipedia*, a research guide that is a crowdsourced wealth of information available to anyone at no cost. One of the benefits of technology is the ability to work with others unlike ourselves. From people of diverse culture, thought, or even character we can develop our own *cultural literacy* using the power of technology to gain access to people from around the world. Finally, the use of technology requires *character* as we face near-term issues of free speech and the longer-term power of artificial intelligence.

Just as demonstrated by Will Talley, the power of technology is in your hands to empower your individual learning journey. He was able to leverage all nine critical success factors *and* the power of technology to advance his academic journey all the way to Harvard. Whether you are a student in high school, a college graduate trying to decide on your next academic or career move, or simply a retiree looking for a more interesting way to fill the day; the power of technology is in your hands as an enabler to learn.

CHAPTER 15

LIFELONG LEARNING: BECOMING A RENAISSANCE PERSON

"I am still learning"

Michelangelo (at age 87)

When you think of your educational journey, it is likely your experience in an institutionalized setting immediately comes to mind. From early learning to middle school, then high school, and—for many—college or post-graduate training, we are mostly familiar with education through the classroom. However, when that portion of your journey comes to an end, a new one begins, the pursuit of lifelong learning. While we garner much from a classroom, that is only one piece of the learning pie. The remainder of the pie is a combination of what we do outside of the classroom. That, in many ways, is where curiosity and a thirst for knowledge come into play.

Formal education is a clearly defined journey. For most, by your mid-twenties you will have exhausted your institutionalized ride. At that point, many of us believe we're done. We've finished our education and then move on with the business of life. Without the structure or possibly the discipline of a formal education environment, some of us simply stop. Is there a lesson plan for life? Where does humanity go to school?

Throughout the evolution of humanity, the Renaissance period (roughly from the fourteenth to the sixteenth century) is recognized as a period driven by cultural, artistic, political, and economic rebirth after the Middle Ages. This period of intellectual reawakening and rapid advancement for humanity was not fueled by traditional education. The modern classroom didn't exist and most of the great minds of the era were self-taught, driven by intellectual curiosity and a lifelong passion for learning.

Leonardo da Vinci became the prototypical "Renaissance man" through his own drive for intellectual curiosity. Sometimes the Renaissance man is thought of as a polymath, one who has deep knowledge about a variety of subjects. It is not just knowledge but a passion for and competence in a few fields that makes one more talented, productive, and certainly more interesting. The concept of the Renaissance man comes from a reference to the most talented artists, scientists, and thinkers who lived during the fourteenth to seventeenth centuries. Self-taught in the arts and sciences, da Vinci was a painter, an architect, a mathematician, and a scientist, interested in learning anything about the universe, including our place in it. Within his notebooks we see evidence of this curiosity. How do birds fly? Why is the sky blue? Why do people yawn? This curiosity drove his science, his math, and his art.

His drawings included detailed sketches of flying machines that would precede human flight by nearly four hundred years! What set da Vinci apart is not his native genius. Yes, he was probably a person of unusually high intelligence. Rather, his curious mind was his most pronounced characteristic. Born into poverty, he never had access to traditional education, but his obsession with knowledge drove him to be self-taught across all disciplines. This is a common theme and practice of the Renaissance, a fervent period of European cultural, artistic, political, and economic rebirth following the Middle Ages.

The Renaissance promoted the rediscovery of classical philosophy, literature, and art. The basic idea of the Renaissance person is not only within Renaissance Europe but carried over into the United States and into modern times. Benjamin Franklin, Thomas Jefferson, and other contemporaries could all be characterized as lifelong learners whose knowledge spanned the arts and sciences, resulting in huge contributions to society.

One of their contemporaries, who was driven by endless curiosity, is an unsung hero named Benjamin Banneker. The son of former slaves, Banneker worked on the family tobacco farm and was largely self-educated. His highly developed intellect came from reading. He became a voracious reader of mathematics, astronomy, and every book that he could borrow from friends and neighbors. At fifteen years old, he took over the family farm and developed an irrigation system to manage water flow from nearby springs. The farm prospered because of his innovative approach. Rather than enjoying his prosperity, Banneker continued to learn. After borrowing a pocket watch from a wealthy acquaintance, he created a fully working clock out of carved wooden parts that became the first clock made in America and led to the creation of his own timekeeping business.

After studying astronomy, he accurately predicted a solar eclipse in 1789 and became a writer, publishing an almanac and ephemeris of Pennsylvania, Virginia, Delaware, and Maryland for over a decade. Banneker sent the almanac to Jefferson along with a strong reproach of slavery. Already an accomplished surveyor, Jefferson invited him to be part of a surveying team selected to lay out Washington, DC. When the team fell into disarray, Banneker stepped in to save the project and is credited for designing the urban layout that we proudly call our nation's capital.

This is the ultimate expression of "education is freedom"—when the son of slaves can become a respected inventor, scientist, and architect using his self-taught education to contribute to the foundation of our country. This desire to learn, acquire information, and reinvent yourself is what drives education and curiosity. Examples of this exist everywhere, even today.

A Renaissance person never stops learning. They rarely become complacent, accepting the status quo. Think of the most interesting person you know. There is one common denominator. That person, driven by intellectual curiosity, likely has knowledge of a place, a people, a skill, or a topic that you find intriguing. Intellectual curiosity drives some people to great achievements while leaving others, remote in hand, to be entertained. Is it a thirst for knowledge, a curious mind, or the emotion of discovery that drives us?

Going back to that eureka moment I experienced while walking across the campus of Columbia University many years ago, I will never forget that chance encounter with the young man wearing a T-shirt that boldly proclaimed, "Education Is Freedom." That was one of those "God winks" moments that stopped me cold. Until that moment, I thought I was done with education. I thought my learning journey was complete and that I was on track toward a successful career. But in that unexpected moment, I realized that my learning journey had just begun. While grateful that my formal education had given me the tools to learn, and I also realized that it was time to put those tools to work to continue to expand my horizons—my freedom—by pursuing a path of lifelong learning.

It can be humbling to realize there is so much more. Seeing learning as a journey rather than a destination makes it easier to sit back and enjoy the ride. Consider this example: As a child, I wanted to be an astronaut. During the Apollo missions, I would sit inside a cardboard box with dials and switches drawn in crayon and imagine myself at the controls of the lunar module as we descended to the surface of the moon. Well, I fell a bit short of this goal, but as an old saying goes, "aim for the stars and you still may achieve the moon." Being a pilot ended up being my personal aerospace learning journey. As soon as I could afford flying lessons, I began to learn to fly. This was no small task because the cost of training allowed me to fly only occasionally, when I could save up enough for the next lesson. At this stage, many new pilots give up. The training is difficult, sometimes scary, and always expensive.

Many people give up before completing the typical forty hours it takes to become a private pilot. I never gave up. I spread my training over many years to afford the lessons. I had to save up for each one, so it felt like I was starting over every time I got into an aircraft, sometimes months since the previous lesson. It was a cumulative process of learning and a journey that continues today, accomplished one small step at a time. Eventually, I purchased an old beat-up Beechcraft Bonanza that gave me lots of experience, sometimes with a few scares along the way. When I had to sell the Bonanza to pay the bills, my wife insisted that I get back in the air. She surprised me one birthday with a few hours of helicopter training to satisfy my need to fly.

The learning continued. I went on to earn a helicopter rating, eventually getting back into fixed-wing planes. I learned to fly twin engines; trained to become instrument rated so that I could fly in any weather; earned my float plane rating on Lake Como, Italy; and even learned classic stick and rudder flying in a classic World War II trainer called the AT-6 Texan. Over time I progressed to earn a type-rating with single pilot certification in a Citation CE-525 business jet. Today, I have the same annual training as professional pilots in the cockpit of the airlines. I have the privilege of being licensed to fly single-pilot (yes, without even a copilot) in a jet aircraft at forty-five thousand feet. This aviation journey has been a lifelong investment in learning. Looking out the cockpit window at a sky that is a deeper blue than one can see from the ground with the sight of a slight curvature of the earth and the majesty of our country passing below…well, in those instances, I can't help but say a small prayer of gratitude. And who knows, one day I may have that opportunity to free myself from the surly bonds of earth and travel in space. Education is indeed freedom!

APPLICATION OF LIFELONG LEARNING

In so many ways, lifelong learning has continued to enrich my own freedom and can do the same for you. You don't have to pursue becoming a pilot. You can literally do anything that piques your interests and drives your passion. Perhaps you want to take up golf or tennis, learn to bake or make homemade pasta, ride a motorcycle, paint, or play an instrument. The choice is yours. In addition to realizing a new hobby or interest, the pursuit of knowledge keeps your mind sharp and keeps you on a lifelong journey to improve and elevate your existence. There are as many ways to learn as there are grains of sand on the beach. The power of lifelong learning is remarkable. I have witnessed and experienced it firsthand. To that end, consider these real-world examples of careers and industries that must adapt to constant change. Within each of these fields, the lifelong pursuit of knowledge pays remarkable dividends to all:

> *Leadership*: I have the privilege, from time to time, to teach aspiring business students about leadership. There are countless books available, but I prefer to teach from experience. One constant in leadership that management gurus often overlook is the importance of responding to change. Leadership isn't a static skill. It is dynamic. Teams change, interpersonal behaviors within a team will change, the fundamentals of business will change, competitive forces will change, and so forth. We hear about servant leadership, managing by walking around, and on and on, but we don't hear enough about the reality that leadership *requires* change. The leader must adapt to the changing dynamics which requires continuous learning. Therefore, leadership is about learning.
>
> *Teaching*: Ultimately, we are all teachers. Whether we teach our children, our employees, or students in the classroom, at some point we will all be placed in a position of responsibility to teach someone else. Teacher education is a formalized process that

hasn't changed significantly in the past one hundred years. It is a noble profession, and we should all be grateful to those who have committed their lives to teaching others. It clearly isn't for the money or even for the notoriety. It is for the love of students and the respect for their profession that teachers give so freely of themselves for so little in return. Just as with leadership, teaching is a dynamic process. What worked in last year's class may not work next year. We must recognize the need to adapt and modify our approach to meet the changing needs or circumstances of the times. Teachers are the ultimate, lifelong learning machines.

Computer Programming: When I studied programming in college (COBOL and Fortran languages), we sat at terminals keying in code to be punched into a huge deck of cards that would then be slowly inserted into a massive computing device. That device would then decode this series of ones and zeros to spit out a program and create a computer-driven result. This clumsy process convinced me at an early age that programming was not a skill that I wanted to perfect. By the time I took my first job, I enjoyed an advantage in the workplace by using a new "portable computer," a very clunky and limited device, but it was being driven by a new kind of software called DOS that allowed me to bypass the old punch cards and to key instructions directly into the software. My point? Computer programming is the ultimate form of lifelong learning because it is always changing and improving. This requires constant learning by anyone in the profession to keep up with the latest changes and adapt to new styles of learning and programming. Even machine learning, or artificial intelligence, is an indication of the importance of lifelong learning. We have something to learn from artificial intelligence that applies to "real" intelligence; it is a dynamic process of learning that continues indefinitely.

Health Care: Nurses, doctors, dentists, and others whom we rely on to take care of our health needs are all engaged in career-long learning. Most are required to take regular refresher courses and learn the latest medical practices. If we think about the huge improvements in health care over the past century, we can thank the continued diligence of our health care professionals in their dedication to continued learning as they practice their craft. Since we all may one day rely on the service of a health care professional, we should be grateful for their professional commitment to continued learning.

Aviation Professionals: Learning to be a pilot may seem daunting, but it is a profession in increasingly high demand. It is also a profession that doesn't require a college degree but does, however, require a continued commitment to learning. Earning a private pilot's certificate simply requires forty hours of flight training, some ground school, and a little practice. Once earning that certificate, however, a pilot is basically licensed to learn. It is the actual experience of flying the aircraft in various conditions (wind, rain, clouds, etc.) that makes a pilot safe. It is also a continued path through instrument training, dual engine training, and specific type ratings that allow pilots to fly more advanced aircraft over time. Even when trained, a commercial pilot must retrain at least once (maybe twice) per year. During that training, they must pass a written exam and a flight test to demonstrate continued proficiency. A pilot is always learning, and we should be grateful, as passengers, to their dedication to the craft.

Agriculture/Farmers: One of the most noble professions is accomplished by those who carve a living from the dirt and make it possible for all of us to eat. We think of farming as a simple job. Till soil, plant the seed, water the crop, harvest the crop, and sell the product. Easy, right? The reality is that the conditions for farmers change daily. Good weather and bad; torrential rainstorms or droughts; disease or varmints; commodity pricing that can make a grown farmer cry—all are the elements of change that will make or break a farmer's ability to succeed.

Sarah Frey is known as the Pumpkin Queen because she is not only a successful farmer and entrepreneur, but the largest pumpkin grower in the country. Sarah says it best in a quote from her book, *The Growing Season*: "Everything is seasonal. You have dark times and bright ones. For human beings, every season can be a growing season. The ones that are fallow can teach you as much as the ones that are bountiful." Frey has become a success by learning and adapting to change.

These are simply a few examples of the power of lifelong learning to transform the trajectory of one's career. Often, we forget how much learning can factor into one's success in any role. A plumber, a farmer, a banker, and a baker will all benefit from a continued focus on honing the skills of their trade and continuing to learn throughout their career. While it may seem obvious that the more you know, the more you can succeed, we often get busy with our day-to-day lives and forget the importance of growth. That growth can, and should, extend beyond simply our profession of choice.

BREADTH AND DEPTH OF KNOWLEDGE

When it comes to education and the acquisition of knowledge, we can either go wide (breadth) or go deep (depth) in our pursuit of learning. Wisdom, or true knowledge, lies at the intersection of knowing and experiencing a great many things. This is the very nature of a liberal arts education. The *Merriam-Webster* definition of the liberal arts references "college or university studies (such as language, philosophy, literature, abstract science) intended to provide chiefly general knowledge and to develop general intellectual capacities (such as reason and judgment) as opposed to professional or vocational skills."

In his book, *In Defense of a Liberal Education,* Fareed Zakaria cites a 2013 survey from the American Association of Colleges and Universities. It reports that 74 percent of employers would recommend a good liberal arts education to students as the best way to prepare for today's ever-changing global economy. When we have a broader base of understanding, we have an ability to keep an open mind to consider others' ideas. We can also draw from more tools to find improved solutions to problems across a broad spectrum. Zakaria also notes that one of the more enduring strengths of a liberal arts education is that it "broadens" us; that exposure to literature, history, science, music, and other arts, he states, will prepare us for a richer personal life. "A liberal education," he says, "gives us greater capacity to be good workers but it will also give us the capacity to be good partners, friends, parents, and citizens." I readily attribute the breadth of my own learning interests to my liberal arts education at the College of the Holy Cross. Specialization in business learning came through graduate school, but the ability to think, to learn, and to communicate effectively came from a solid liberal arts foundation.

The beauty of learning is that it comes in all shapes and sizes. For example, physical activity has been linked to learning and to longevity. Many of us remember the days of physical education classes in school, wearing some very awkward looking gym clothes. Dr. John Ratey, an associate clinical professor of psychiatry at Harvard Medical School, has written extensively about the benefits of exercise improving learning on three levels: "First," he said, "it optimizes your mind-set to improve alertness, attention, and motivation; second, it prepares and encourages nerve cells to bind to one another, which is the cellular basis for logging in new information; and third, it spurs the development of new nerve cells from stem cells in the hippocampus." Another noted physician and fitness expert, Dr. Kenneth

Cooper, is best known as the "Father of Aerobics." Dr. Cooper and his Cooper Institute have for many decades researched the positive correlation between physical fitness and academic performance and overall better cognitive function.

Exercise not only prepares the brain to get ready to learn, but it makes retaining information easier. Exercise and physical activity are an essential component to lifelong learning. Whether tennis, golf, paddleball, or any sport that we can play long into our lives, the more we learn the more fun we can have. The more fun we have, then the more we will exercise and extend not only our mental capacity but our very physical existence. Another one of the hidden benefits of lifelong learning is to live longer!

Perhaps you aren't an athlete but have a love for the arts, like music. Do you listen to music in a mindless way, or do you learn from music? Most of us do a little of both. Music often sets the mood, but how many times do you really listen to the beats, the instruments, and the lyrics? Music appreciation is another form of learning. Today's technology allows us to listen to music in very different ways. We can pull up a score and watch as we listen, following the beat as the notes pass by. We can pull up the lyrics and read as we listen to the poetry of song in our ears. Each of these exercises provides a new appreciation for the music that we are hearing. It is all part of our learning process as we expand our music appreciation horizons. If we wish to take it to another level, we can learn to play music at virtually any age. It isn't necessary to be a concert pianist to appreciate the sound of a chord progression or a simple melody. All of this is possible with a little training and a healthy dose of desire. It isn't difficult to learn to play music. It is difficult to start. Once you begin, you will realize the joy that it can bring to anyone at any age.

Visual art has also been integral to humanity since the beginning of time when cave drawings communicated and preserved stories of human culture for generations never imagined. But what is art, and why does it seem that some of us can appreciate only one genre or format? Consider the difference between these two famous masters:

Leonardo da Vinci's *Mona Lisa* is almost lifelike in its realism. In stark contrast, Kazimir Malevich's *Black Square* is just that, a stark black square on white canvas. Both extremes are considered masterpieces. Next, consider the works inside the Museum of Modern Art (MoMA). A trip to the MoMA, will expose you to a range of art, from a box of rocks to a blank wall with a crack running through it.

In this context, we are all art lovers. We all have an innate desire to enjoy the beauty and the expressionism of art, and yet many of us are afraid to venture beyond that which we know. An important part of lifelong learning is the freedom of unleashing our art aesthete or even our inner artist. Touring a new museum with an experience guide or even picking up a paintbrush and putting color on canvas can be freeing. Visiting a sculpture garden or even molding a lump of clay into a bowl can be another richly rewarding experiences. As with any other form of learning, we start with the basics or fundamentals and then progress with more learning and more practical experience. The one given is that our reward from experiencing the visual arts will be a broadening of the richness of life.

Have you ever wanted to communicate freely with others in their native tongue? Traveling in another country and speaking to people there in their language or even communicating with someone down the street in their native tongue is one of the greatest expressions of freedom for humankind. Reaching another human in their place, in their language, creates another level of understanding and intimacy that only those with multi-language skills can comprehend. Learning another language unlocks many doors, from cultural understanding to ease of navigation.

With the many tools available today, language learning is as simple as a few minutes a day with an app such as Babbel or Rosetta Stone. These tools allow us to learn the way we did as children though visual association of places and things and then progressing through simple conversations. As with any form of learning, it is simply a matter of willingness and time before we find ourselves able to communicate in another language. A trip to explore the wonders of Patagonia as an English-speaking tourist can never compare to the richness of speaking Spanish with the locals, another example of education enriching your personal freedom.

THE IMPACT OF LIFELONG LEARNING ON OUR SOCIETY

We are surrounded with opportunities to learn, to expand our horizons, and to take on new and curious experiences. Ranging from music to art to literature to social media, each of these outlets gives us a tremendous outlet to pursue knowledge. Yes, even social media provides a vehicle to learn. But social media is often a mindless journey. How many hours do we burn by scrolling through page after page of personal updates or videos that are carefully curated by an AI algorithm to keep our attention or to direct us to other mindless forms of entertainment?

This mindless entertainment is no different from the forms of distraction that we've had for generations. Paging through magazines, watching hour after hour of television shows, or listening to music as background noise are all examples of entertainment activities that do little to enrich our lives. If we take the same basic mediums and simply apply a different approach, we can turn mindless entertainment into mindful learning.

Next time you're scrolling through one hundred fifty channel options for television entertainment, consider a documentary that will not only entertain but also teach. Instead of the romance novel that may provide mindless relaxation on a flight, consider a literary classic or perhaps a historical novel. Even social media can have redeeming value when mindless scrolling is replaced with a targeted search to find specific topics that provide an opportunity for mindful learning. It is all possible and often at our fingertips. Lifelong learning is everywhere around us; the only obstacle is our willingness to find it and partake of it. But maybe the most important point to this chapter is that we all benefit from collective learning.

Helping our students get the right education from the beginning and then fostering a culture of lifelong learning is the best antidote to the challenges that humanity faces. As Gandhi said, "Live as if you were to die tomorrow. Learn as if you were to live forever." Knowledge will ultimately affect every aspect of our lives, from the politicians who govern to the policemen and policewomen who protect. The more they know, the more effective they can be. The more knowledge can shine a light on uncertainty, eliminate fear, and take away our doubts, the safer we will be and the more freedom we will have. Education is, indeed, our freedom.

CHAPTER 16

WISDOM: THE RX FOR HUMANITY

"There is nothing noble in being superior to your fellow man; true nobility is being superior to your former self."

Ernest Hemingway

If learning and knowledge are the antidote to many of society's ills, then why does mankind still suffer from basic societal issues like poverty, crime, racism, bigotry, and other significant issues that still plague us? Even more surprising is the degree to which the most highly educated, developed countries still experience these problems. Tragically, the fight for freedom and fundamental human rights are central issues that continue to fuel ideological fractures, violence, and world wars. The more we learn, it seems, the less we know.

If education is the ultimate answer to societal challenges, then how does one explain the dynamics that led to World War II? Two of its participants, Germany and Japan, were countries that embraced education and were arguably among the most knowledgeable societies in the world when they decided to team up and spark a war that spanned years and multiple countries. While this may seem like ancient history to most, it was not even a hundred years ago—during the 1940s—that millions of highly educated people were willing to do the unthinkable.

It is incomprehensible today that Adolf Hitler was successful in advancing his nationalist vision of Germans as a superior race. More incomprehensible was the willingness of educated German officers to carry out his orders to eradicate the Jewish people. Shouldn't education and knowledge allow human beings to rise above such unthinkable behaviors? If we are truly an educated society, how could this ever occur?

I have posed this question to many learned people and have received a consistent answer. What is lacking they say, is wisdom. While *knowledge* is the accumulation of information and facts through learning, *wisdom* is the ability to apply that knowledge in a meaningful way. It is wisdom that can set us apart from others and substantially reduce the impact of those societal issues.

In an earlier chapter, we explored the dangers of "false knowledge" or the spread of blatantly untrue narratives. Despite our advanced mental abilities, humans are also vulnerable to a tribal-like behavior that may cause us to put our own beliefs aside in the interest of conforming to the wishes of a larger group. We also explored the dangers of "militant ignorance" that causes us to lock down on a subset of information that supports our view of right versus wrong. That is, at least in part, how we can begin to explain the Holocaust. Hate, bigotry, and systemic antisemitism also paint a vivid picture. While our intellect may tell us that something doesn't feel right, our desire to belong or fit in can overpower our intellect and create behaviors that are inconsistent with rational thought. The impact of authority figures on individuals may sometimes replace rational thinking and wisdom with a desire to obey. As far-fetched as this may seem in today's world of individualism, the human instinct to obey can be quite strong. In the 1960s, psychologist Stanley Milgram conducted a series of experiments in an attempt to understand the atrocities committed under the Nazi regime during WWII.

He conducted a series of experiments in which unknowing participants were asked to administer punishment in the form of electric shock to individuals who failed to correctly respond to a predetermined set of questions. The Milgram experiment revealed that a surprising 62 percent of individuals were willing to follow the instructions of the authority figure and administer the highest level of shock that had been defined as "Danger: Severe Shock." Even when the participants were within earshot of the screams and cries for help, the majority still willingly administered the most severe shock.

Milgram's experiments provided insight that may help us understand behaviors that drove many involved with Nazi persecutions. While explaining the vulnerability of human behavior to authority figures, many social scientists believe that the behavior of individuals goes beyond a simple response to authority. Those individuals may actually believe they are morally *right* because they are in compliance with an authority figure. Others become selective in their choice of information that makes up their individual base of knowledge. Stephen Hawking, a theoretical physicist, portrayed his cosmic view of knowledge in this powerful quote: "The greatest enemy of knowledge is not ignorance. It is the illusion of knowledge."

Ironically, while many wars have been fought in the name of freedom, this behavior is anything but an expression of a free mind. Jean-Jacques Rousseau, an eighteenth-century French philosopher, noted that "man is born free, and everywhere he is in chains." He tried to explain how freedom is curtailed in several ways. The most obvious is physical constraint. Even in the most freedom-focused societies, the power of the masses may indeed limit our personal freedom. He went on to describe three types of chains that inevitably limit our lives and ability to be free:

> *Physical chains* are bonds that hold us captive. These cannot be easily escaped physically, but mentally we can escape with our mindsets. We can achieve freedom from physical chains by not letting thoughts or impressions hold our minds captive. Senator John McCain described his time in the "Hanoi Hilton"—a nick-

name given by American prisoners of war to Hoa Lò Prison—as physically abusive. Certainly his liberty was constrained. What the North Vietnamese were never able to control in McCain or his fellow American POWs was their mind or their thoughts. Their mental fortitude and intellectual strength enabled these brave men to endure.

Societal chains are customs, mores, or laws that may restrict what we can physically do. This could also be the power of the majority that may impose rules or behaviors that are inconsistent with our personal desires or beliefs. Societal chains can be more difficult to break. In a democracy, the best solution to create change is the power of your vote. Even then, there may be circumstances of the majority to which you can't abide. In these circumstances, one still has choice. One can go along with the masses or speak out for what one believes. Ultimately, one may choose to leave the state or even the country to preserve the integrity of their personal beliefs and to exercise their personal freedom.

Mental chains are the most oppressive threats to our personal liberty and are the focus of this book. They are the self-imposed limitations that sometimes prevent each of us from fulfilling our ultimate goals. Mental chains are the unconscious bonds that restrict what we believe we can do. They are also the blind spots that cause us to follow rather than to lead. Our mental chains sometimes cause us to do things to conform to our tribe, even if our intellect knows better. Sadly, these are the most pervasive chains and the most difficult to escape. These are the deep-seated and firmly established chains that social conditioning often creates. They tell us what we can or can't accomplish. When we make them our reality, our lives turn into an inescapable prison.

Each of these chains rightfully creates limitations on where you go, what you do, and, of course, your quality of life. However, you—

as the individual experiencing life—are armed with a remarkable ability to free yourself from these chains.

> So, if these constraints to freedom are so pervasive, then what *is* the Rx for Humanity?
>
> Where *does* humanity go to school?
>
> How does humanity overcome these physical, societal, and mental constraints?
>
> Is *education* really the answer to *freedom*?

The answer to all these questions is within each of us as individuals and as members of society at large. Humanity cannot address its own limitations, but we as individuals can. This begins with each of us, with the mantra that no human should be left behind. The Rx for humanity is comprised of four essential parts. I would characterize these elements as the culmination of education, and the transformation of *knowledge* into *wisdom*:

1. Overcoming the tyranny of our minds
2. Practicing relentless positivity
3. Owning humility
4. Living a life with compassion

Each of the nine steps in the C-Suite Learnings, as previously outlined, may provide the fundamental tools to navigate these four parts of our Rx, but knowledge alone will not create lasting change. While educated, our society has proven that we can still be our own worst enemy. From the Romans to the Incas, empires have succumbed to their own interests when they forget the Rx for humanity. History continues to repeat itself, but it is time to break the cycle and put this powerful remedy to use. Knowledge is the remedy for a great deal of challenges we face but not necessarily the cure for all of humanity's ills. That takes a collective approach, with each of us doing our part. As we increase our knowledge and actively utilize it, we begin to demonstrate wisdom. Chip Conley, a *New York Times* bestselling author, writes that "wisdom is metabolized experience that leads to distilled compassion." In other words, it is not just learning from our mistakes and historical shortcomings. Rather, it is the act of assuring that our mistakes will lead to more wisdom and an increased inclination toward social good.

OVERCOMING THE TYRANNY OF OUR MINDS

Our peers, family, or environment can create our mental chains. In many cases, we are born into them, or the circumstances of our early years may establish them. This is the little voice in our heads telling us we "can't" succeed or that we aren't smart enough or good enough or aren't worthy. We *must* eliminate these self-imposed restrictions so that we can achieve freedom.

But how do we do this? How can we escape these mental chains that have caused so many problems throughout our lives? The chains that have limited us? Knocked us down? That is where knowledge comes into play. These chains are powerful, but *wisdom* is the ultimate force of nature.

Education is the antidote, enabling us to learn that we are capable and that we can succeed despite any constraints, mental or otherwise. Human nature dictates that we subconsciously move away from things that are dangerous, difficult, or painful and instead move toward things that are easy, painless, and pleasurable. Naturally, we move away from pain and toward pleasure; we look for easier experiences. You will never escape chains if you settle for the status quo. These chains, whether physical, societal, or mental, often result from fear. We are afraid when held hostage, either physically or emotionally, by those around us. Mental chains are the result of our own insecurity, our own fear. Ultimately, *fear* is the most pervasive threat to our collective or individual freedom. So, we must extinguish the fear to usher in the light. Knowledge helps us shine that light, but wisdom extinguishes the fear.

Self-determination of a people, whether the American people or the people of the world, must begin with "self." We each have a choice: we can accept obstacles, negative influences, and adversity and wallow in despair and hopelessness, or we can take responsibility for our own destiny by living our fullest lives and making our greatest contributions to the world around us. Even with knowledge, we may still be afraid. But with wisdom, we can be positive of a brighter day ahead.

PRACTICING RELENTLESS POSITIVITY

While many paths lead to abating fear and unlocking the chains that constrain our freedom, I find one to be particularly powerful and useful, especially in the context of our conversation in this book. Whether it is physical imprisonment and you're locked away in jail, a societal imprisonment that makes you unhappy with your place in society, or certain mental constraints that create negative thoughts, consider the value of relentless positivity. Relentless positivity caused Nelson Mandela and his peers to study law while imprisoned in South Africa for their political beliefs. It caused Abraham Lincoln to lead the United States through a civil war. It inspired Elon Musk and Jeff Bezos to believe they could reinvent their respective industries...and led both to believe they could help humankind reach for the stars.

The concept of positivity is sometimes dismissed as Pollyannaish. We must recognize that pain and suffering are real and that we cannot brush away mental health issues with simply an admonition like "don't worry, be happy." Instead, positivity must become an almost innate ability to see our pain through a lens of compassion and with an attitude of hope. Only when we look inward with self-caring can we understand that our brain health will be better served with joy than despair. We should hold up this same lens up for others, to be compassionate about their suffering but to do our best to share an attitude of relentless positivity that may project hope.

One of my favorite quotes is from Martin Luther King: "We must accept finite disappointment, but never lose infinite hope." Hope and positivity often go hand in hand, one often the product of the other. In both his personal life and his public life, Dr. King endured many challenges. He could easily have been filled with negativity and self-doubt. Instead, he accepted those challenges and setbacks, recognizing them as part of the journey toward what he called "the Promised Land." As a result, he was freed to accept his own failures in the confidence that progress was being made and that hope would help him prevail. The most knowledgeable of men can be positive, but only the wisest of men will be humble.

IT MAY BE HARD TO BE HUMBLE, BUT HUMILITY WINS

If we look at the toxicity of today's rhetoric, the divisive and often hurtful polarization of our politics has divided even friends and families. People have a hard time listening to each other. They have little respect for those with whom they disagree. They don't take diverging views seriously. Often, we have so much self-confidence in our own opinions that we are unable to be self-critical, so the idea that others hold different opinions becomes disturbing, almost a personal affront.

Throughout our history, however, the greatest leaders have often been the most humble. Abraham Lincoln was known for assembling a "team of rivals," being humble enough to respect his opponents and learn from them. He knew listening to the opposition would offer him insights and perspectives that might shape his own efforts and decisions. When the great orator, abolitionist, and former slave Frederick Douglass viciously criticized President Lincoln for his willingness to return escaped slaves to their owners, Lincoln invited Douglass to the White House for a chat. By listening to one another, and showing respect for their divergent beliefs, the two men eventually became close friends. Frederick Douglass's involvement in Lincoln's administration ultimately helped shape the Emancipation Proclamation. Lincoln was humble enough to listen to and show respect for his harshest critic.

Those who are most humble recognize that they don't know everything or understand everything. They see that their opinions are indeed opinions and that there is seldom only one "right" way to believe. The humble see the world as a vast and complex place that is a constant reminder of how little we know and how much more we must learn. This awe and gratitude ultimately shape our humility, encouraging us to listen to others and to respect their ideas.

COMPASSION: DEVELOPING MUTUAL RESPECT

If we look at today's political landscape, it is easy to see the complete lack of understanding, communication, and compassion that abounds. Across the globe and sometimes across town, society has been carved into sides. This isn't just nationalism causing one country to take sides against another. Even within countries or sometimes even within families, people have become tribal in their polarized views. Ironically, religion or education can sometimes motivate much of this division. One religion takes a stand against another or the intelligentsia in a standoff with the populists. Too often we find that neither side shows compassion toward the other.

The irony is that virtually all religions, despite their differences, have one common theme: They are grounded in a need for compassion toward one's fellow man. How, then, does one explain holy wars, the Crusades, or Jihad? Is it right to put compassion for your fellow man aside in the name of religion? In this context, a "holy war" is a form of oxymoron. Compassion, in its most simplistic terms, is an empathic understanding of another person's feelings. It is often accompanied by a desire to act on that person's behalf. When we look at many of society's issues, ranging from homelessness to immigration to crime, we see bipartisan blame and accusation. At the same time, we see little in the way of collaborative solutions and even less in the way of compassion.

In day-to-day life, we witness acts of compassion every day. If someone drops a bag of groceries, several people will stop to help and pick it up. While easy for an individual to extend kindness, it becomes more difficult for society to impart collective kindness. In other words, as individuals it is easy to be kind and show compassion, but once we retreat into our groups, we can sometimes become less sensitive to the needs of others outside of the immediate group. While compassion implies that you see yourself in another's shoes, a group has no shoes and collective compassion is less likely. As a result, we sometimes put community over compassion and give up our personal kindness while taking on the beliefs of the larger group.

Once we are aware of this vulnerability to override compassion, we are better equipped to make our own choices and to have a favorable influence on the decisions of the whole. Ultimately, compassion is kindness rooted in an appreciation of other human beings as real people who also suffer. With knowledge comes understanding. With understanding comes compassion. With compassion comes kindness. With kindness, humanity will have a greater chance of success. In this sense, education *is* freedom *and* it is an Rx for humanity. It is not just the power of knowledge, but the transformation of that knowledge into wisdom that will make us individually and collectively most free. With wisdom, we can spread our wings and fly.

TAKE FLIGHT

Yes, I believe we can fly. I believe that knowledge and ultimately our wisdom will allow us to enjoy whatever freedom and whatever adventure life has to offer. If this sounds like relentless or unbridled positivity, it is. Simply put, it is a manifestation of the "gift." This C-Suite of Learning, the cumulative benefit of these nine success factors, will bear the gift of *wisdom* and ultimately the gift of freedom.

Change does not define us but rather our response to change will establish who we are and how people see us. *Confidence*, of course, goes hand in hand with preparation. *Clarity* helps us communicate, listen, and learn. *Critical thinking* allows us to determine truth from fiction to make better choices. *Curiosity* will allow us to open new windows and doors to see what is on the other side. *Creativity* will allow our intellect to have fun and to explore, pushing our own boundaries in fearless fashion. Through *collaboration* we will see and feel the collective benefit of interaction. *Cultural literacy* will help us learn from and appreciate those who are different from us. Finally, our *character* will clearly be shaped by the relentless positivity that stems from all the above. These are the elements of wisdom that can define you.

I hope you will make this *your* gift, a gift you can freely share with others. I like to believe that I am a product of the cumulative positivity of all those whom I have encountered in life, taking a little bit of their quality with me along the way and making it my own. If others see you in that fashion, they too will wish to take a part of you with them and to help you succeed. With absolute confidence, I believe I can do this, you can do this, and collectively *we* can do this to make this world a better place.

Now that you have the gift, it is up to you to use it. Where do you start? Well, all good teachers, from Abraham to Socrates to Jesus to Muhammad, used parables to help their students learn. In that esteemed tradition, I will leave you with one of my favorites:

In a small village there lived a wise elder to whom everyone turned for guidance and advice. One day, a young boy decided to confront the gentleman with a question that he knew could not be answered. His plan? To find a small butterfly and hold it cupped in his hands, hidden from sight. He would then approach the man and ask him to guess what he had buried in his hands.

If answered correctly, he would then ask the zinger: Was the butterfly alive or dead?

If the wise one said the butterfly was alive, the boy would crush the butterfly with his hands and thereby prove the elder wrong. But if the gentleman said it was dead, the boy would open his hands and let the butterfly fly free, demonstrating at last that the elder was not as wise as everyone thought him to be.

So, the boy ventured off and found a small butterfly that fit neatly within his hands. As he approached the gentleman, the boy said, "Wise sir, can you tell what I have in my hands?"

"Why of course I can," the elder responded without hesitation. "From the net you have in your back pocket it is plain to see it is a small butterfly that you have cradled in your hands."

"Ah, that is so," the young boy exclaimed, "but is the butterfly alive or dead?"

The wise man paused, then rubbed his chin in contemplation. Looking the young boy in the eyes, he replied in a soft tone, "Whether the butterfly is

> alive or dead *is in your hands* my child. The choice is yours."

Wisdom...is in your hands! The choice is yours! I hope you have enjoyed this journey and will choose to make education your freedom, knowing with confidence that freedom too is in your hands. With education and wisdom, we can spread our wings and fly!

***The future is in your hands*!**

ACKNOWLEDGMENTS

Gratitude is one of the learnings captured in this work. It is with gratitude and humility that I look to those who have guided this journey and made it possible. First, to Stedman Graham, my profound appreciation to you for providing the unrelenting encouragement to make this possible. From your early encouragement and support for the Education is Freedom Foundation to your relentless urging for me to carry this important message to the world, and from your wisdom and guidance in the very structure of this book to your friendship, I am forever grateful. To every member of the Education is Freedom Foundation, from the board to the staff to the many counselors who change lives every day, thank to you for sharing the dream and for making it all possible. Alumni of the Education is Freedom Foundation, like Adan Gonzalez and hundreds of thousands who have come through the program to find their own path, all represent living examples of the freedom that can come from education. Many thanks to each of you for your continued inspiration.

To my friends in the Horatio Alger Association, I am thankful for your many personal experiences that provided such rich context for others to learn. I am forever grateful for Lou Brock, may he rest in peace, for his introduction and subsequent nomination to the Association. Every member in this group of distinguished Americans and every student granted one of the thousands of scholarships represent the power of education and determination to overcome adversity. Each of them is a living example of the power of the American dream.

To the unsung heroes of this world—the teachers who believed in me, encouraged me and, yes, tolerated me—I am grateful for your tireless dedication to changing lives.

To my wife Margo and my entire family, I am forever indebted to you for the unwavering belief in me and for sharing this grand adventure called life. Finally, many thanks to Justin Spizman, the "book architect," and Jan Miller, the "agent of agents," who provided the experience and talent to guide this literary work. And finally, to you, the reader, I am thankful for your trust in giving some small portion of your personal learning journey to share mine. My dream is that everyone who believes that *education is freedom* will choose to pay it forward by passing along their copy, giving additional copies as gifts, or—for those able to do so—providing books to libraries or schools so that young readers all over the world have the freedom to fly!

ABOUT THE AUTHOR

James W. Keyes is a global business leader, philanthropist, educator, artist, musician, commercial rated pilot, and modern renaissance man. He is the former CEO of two internationally recognized Fortune 500 companies, 7-Eleven, Inc. and Blockbuster, Inc. His other business interests cover a broad range of industries from retail, consumer products, technology, healthcare, cyber security, new space, energy, and advanced nuclear. He sits on several public company boards and serves as a board adviser to a venture capital firm and a number of start-up companies. Keyes's philanthropic initiatives have an equally broad focus, including serving a three-term seat on the Board of Governors for the American Red Cross, acting as the former Chairman of the Dallas Symphony Orchestra, and serving on the board of directors for institutions such as UT Southwestern Medical School, Cooper Institute, St. Jude Children's Research Hospital, Dallas Performing Arts Center, SMU Cox School of Business, Columbia Business School, and his alma mater, College of the Holy Cross. He has had a lifelong commitment to education, serving as a founding director of the Dallas Education Foundation and is the founder of the Education Is Freedom Foundation. Keyes is a personification of the American Dream, as he comes from humble beginnings. He was inducted in 2005 as a Member of the Horatio Alger Association of Distinguished Americans.

INFORMATION ON EDUCATION IS FREEDOM FOUNDATION (501C3 NONPROFIT)

EDUCATION *is* FREEDOM

The Education is Freedom Foundation (www.educationisfreedom.org) was the brainchild of Jim Keyes, then President and CEO of 7-Eleven, Inc., on the simple belief that every young person deserves an opportunity to achieve their full potential. When Jim's board of directors suggested a cost saving cut to the company philanthropic gift budget, he began looking for ways to show a return on investment on those dollars to preserve the company's level of giving. Rather than disburse the funds across hundreds of well-intended causes, he identified rising personnel costs and the desire for a diverse workforce as the company's biggest priorities.

What better way to show a return, but to target philanthropic dollars at public schools where the company could grow its own future store operators. He partnered with state and local officials, fellow CEOs and school administrators to create the Education is

Freedom Foundation. At a celebration of 7-Eleven's 75th anniversary, the organization launched at Radio City Music Hall in 2002 with performances by Nelly, JaRule, Juanes, and others including a special keynote message from Nelson Mandela who said "the concept of Education is Freedom will change the world".

In nearly twenty years since its inception, the foundation has helped nearly 500,000 students find their path to higher education. It has also helped these students raise over $300 million in scholarship money to support their higher education dreams. The first in his family to attend college, Jim was able to leverage his education to ultimately lead two Fortune 500 companies.

He remains committed to helping show other less fortunate students the path. Committed to lifelong learning, Jim is the embodiment of the phrase, *Education is Freedom.*

It matters not how straight the gate,

How charged with punishments the scroll,

I am the master of my fate,

I am the captain of my soul.

Invictus by William Ernest Henley

Printed in Great Britain
by Amazon

42769495R00155